George Buchanan

by

John Campbell Smith

Robert Wallace

George Buchanan
by John Campbell Smith
Robert Wallace

Copyright © 2024

All Rights reserved.

ISBN: 978-93-61427-94-7

Published by

DOUBLE 9 BOOKS

2/13-B, Ansari Road
Daryaganj, New Delhi – 110002
info@double9books.com
www.double9books.com
Tel. 011-40042856

ABOUT THE AUTHOR

John Campbell Smith was a Scottish writer, attorney, and Sheriff-Substitute in Forfarshire. He was a typical 'lad o' pairts', a brilliant Scots youth from the nineteenth century who rose from very poor beginnings. Campbell Smith was born in Wellfield, near Leuchars, Fife, on December 12, 1828. His father, John Smith, was a weaver and farmer, while his mother was Anne Campbell. He attended the village subscription school until the age of twelve, when he became an apprentice mason. He worked at that trade until he felt he had acquired enough money to attend university. He left his job in St. Andrews on a Saturday afternoon after saving up enough money.

Robert Wallace was a Scottish historian and biographer renowned for his thorough study and astute analysis. His opus, "George Buchanan," explores the lives and times of the great Scottish humanist and scholar. Wallace's biography paints a complete picture of Buchanan, emphasizing his contributions to literature, politics, and education during the Renaissance period. Wallace's vivid portrait of Buchanan's intellectual pursuits, political activities, and cultural impact is based on a detailed investigation of primary sources and historical records, giving light on his influence on Scottish history and European humanism. Wallace's work continues to make an important contribution to our knowledge of both Buchanan's life and the larger historical context in which he lived.

CONTENTS

PREFACE

The concluding chapter of the book I intended to serve the purpose of prologue and epilogue, but on reflection I find that readers both in and out of Scotland may desire to be told a little more about Robert Wallace, M.A., D.D., and M.P., a collocation of titles of honour, so far as I know, unexampled. He was a minister of the Church of Scotland from the summer of 1857 to the autumn of 1876; was in succession the minister of Newton-on-Ayr, of Trinity College Church, Edinburgh, and of Old Greyfriars', Edinburgh, in which last he succeeded Dr. Robert Lee, as also in the leadership of the Liberal Party of the Church of Scotland. The degree of D.D. was conferred upon him by the University of Glasgow, pretty much, it was believed, through the influence of Dr. Caird, the most eloquent preacher and one of the most profound theologians of our day. After Dr. Wallace became editor of the *Scotsman* he resigned his chair of Church History, his church, and even his licence to preach, and he left in abeyance the title of D.D., and became in his time, as a barrister-at-law, plain Mr. Robert Wallace. But the degree of a university is, I believe, indelible, and he will always be Dr. Wallace to me. His degree of M.A., like mine, was conferred by the University of St. Andrews in April 1853 after four years' study, during which we attended simultaneously every Humanity class. He was first in every literary class, and by far the best classical scholar of my day. Dr. Alexander, the venerable professor of Greek, who had taught for thirty years, pronounced him the best student he had ever taught.

His splendid classical attainments, the erudition necessary to the chair of Church History, his extensive and distinguished practice as a debating gladiator in Church Courts, especially the General Assembly, perhaps even his experience in the solid, stolid, non-mercurial House of Commons, all fitted him, as few men have been fit, to do justice to the life, labours, and supreme European culture of George Buchanan.

To equal fitness I do not pretend. To the best of my ability I have tried to complete the unfinished task of my friend, with whom I at intervals interchanged ideas since the beginning of our college career in October 1849. I am not sure he would have agreed with all I say in the last chapter. For the views expressed therein I alone am responsible.

From one error in fact and a doubtful assumption as to Buchanan's relation to Montaigne, the 'representative' sceptic, I have been saved by Dr. P. Hume Brown, the author of the best life of Buchanan, whose knowledge of the history of Buchanan and his contemporaries is probably unrivalled. He read the proof-sheets, and for his friendly, disinterested attention Dr. Wallace's representatives and I are greatly obliged to him, as all readers ought to be, for they have the assurance that the most enlightened eye on the subject of Buchanan examined what they are expected to believe.

J. CAMPBELL SMITH.

Dundee, *December 1899*.

CHAPTER I
PRELIMINARY AND GENERAL

On the 21st July 1683, Lord William Russell was beheaded in Lincoln's Inn Fields, because Charles II., F.D., who never said a foolish thing, and never did a wise one, thought it would help to keep alive the Stuart doctrine of the Divine right of kings. On the same day, the political writings of George Buchanan and one John Milton were, by decree of the learned and loyal University of Oxford, publicly burned in front of their Schools by the common hangman, because they were regarded as the most formidable and dangerous defences of the principles on account of which it had been considered judicious to kill Lord William Russell, and perhaps also in token that if Buchanan and Milton had not been dead they might have been burned too, along with their books. It is comforting to reflect that this same decree was subsequently burned with the same publicity—and by the same common hangman, one would hope.

At the time, however, the Oxford transaction, in view of the sycophancy, obscurantism, and other degrading characteristics of the then University, was the highest compliment that could have been paid to Buchanan and Milton, and especially to Buchanan. For Buchanan was substantially a century before Milton, who, like the rest of the Roundheads, was inspired by Buchanan's principles and greatly assisted by his arguments. Dryden, indeed, declared that Milton stole his *Defence of the People of England* from Buchanan's *De Jure Regni apud Scotos*; but that was only 'Glorious John's' inglorious way of making himself controversially disagreeable. Milton put his own genius and experience into Buchanan's idea, and produced an essentially original work. But what although he had not? Milton was fighting a great battle, and was entitled, or rather bound, to use the best weapons, wherever he could get them. The anti-plagiarising spirit is often a mere form of vanity. If the Royal Artillery declined to plagiarise from Armstrong and Krupp, and insisted on making all their ammunition themselves, I should tremble for the defence of the country. Not the less, however, does Buchanan amply merit the title of 'Father of Liberalism,' since the principles which he successfully floated in unpropitious times undoubtedly produced the two great English, the American, and the first French Revolutions, with all their continuations and consequences.

Let it be noted that the distinction which Buchanan achieved in this matter was not merely that of the political philosopher and thinker. The publication of the *De Jure*, at the time and under the circumstances in which it appeared, was a blow of the utmost consequence, delivered in the great politico-theological struggle with which he was contemporary. It was like one of Knox's famous sermons, which were not mere religious meditations, but political events of the most immense influence, present and future. The Reformation, particularly in Scotland, was, in its inception and establishment, a political, quite as much as a religious revolution, of which Buchanan was not simply an interested but recluse critic and dilettante spectator. He thought profoundly about what he saw going on, but he also threw his thoughts into the fight that was raging round him, with bombshell results, and the effects of what he thought and did upon the fortunes of the great struggle for popular liberty against usurping ascendency—a struggle not even yet concluded—prove him to have possessed qualities of far-sightedness and statesmanship of the highest order.

In a totally different walk of life he achieved almost equal distinction. He was a great scholar-poet and general writer; and when, in this connection, I use the words 'almost equal,' I am thinking of the question whether the director of human affairs or the artist in words and ideas of beauty or human interest is the greater. Of course, comparison of things or people generically distinct is scarcely possible. You can hardly compare a snuff-box and a policeman. But it seems less difficult to ask whether Cæsar or Shakespeare, Alfred the Great or Alfred Tennyson, was the greater man. However that may be, there can be no doubt that Buchanan rose to very great eminence as an intellectual artist, both in prose and verse. He enjoyed an unsurpassed European reputation among the Renaissance magnates of his day. Henri Estienne, for instance,—Buchanan's Stephanus, our Stephens—said that he was *poetarum nostri sæculi facile princeps*, meaning thereby 'easily the first poet of our time,' which is sufficiently strong. Of course it may be said that Estienne or Stephens was only a printer. But there are printers *and* printers, and Stephanus belonged to the second class. Anybody who knows anything about the literary history of the time will understand that such praise from Estienne implied a very great deal.

Then there were the Scaligers, Julius Cæsar *père*, and Joseph *fils*, a greater man than his father, in the opinion of the best judges—himself included, probably. They were not men easy to please, the Scaligers. Even Erasmus was not good enough for Julius Cæsar, who used language truly awful about the glory of the priesthood and the shame. As for Joseph, there was but one man alive in his own line for whom he had a vestige of respect, and that was Casaubon; and he told him so, intimating that he might think a good deal of the compliment, as he, Joseph, was the only man in Europe who was capable of forming an opinion about him—a perfectly true if not absolutely humble observation. But however difficult to please in most cases, the Scaligers had a sincere and unbounded admiration of Buchanan—an admiration abundantly shown while he lived, and when he was gone, expressed, especially by the younger Scaliger, with a tenderness and beauty which stamp the tribute with authority and value. His epitaphium on Buchanan concluded thus:—

> 'Namque ad supremum perducta Poetica culmen
> In te stat, nec quo progrediatur habet.
> Imperii fuerat Romani Scotia limes;
> Romani eloquii Scotia finis erit.'

Anybody with a fair understanding of Latin and a full understanding of epigram, who reads the last couplet here, will know that Scaliger was perfectly qualified to pronounce a judgment in the matter. For the benefit of the man in the street, it may be stated that what Scaliger was driving at was that Buchanan had brought poetry to a pitch of perfection beyond which it could not go; and that as Scotland had in the past been the last line of expansion for the Roman Empire, so in the future it would, in the person of Buchanan, be found to have given the highest note of Roman eloquence. Of course it may be said that this was only the customary and privileged lie of the epitaph; but that it was really Scaliger's deliberate opinion appears from a well-known quotation from his table-talk, that 'in Latin poetry Buchanan stands alone in Europe, and leaves everybody else behind.' Coming to more modern times, it will probably be admitted that Wordsworth knew good poetry when he saw it, and he says of one of Buchanan's poems—by no means his best—that it was equal in sentiment, if not in elegance, to anything in Horace.

This he said before a pedantic relative pointed out a false quantity. What he would have felt had he known this before he read the poem, Schoolmaster only knows. What the latter potentate would have done we may partly surmise from what Porson actually did when some one got him to commence reading Buchanan's poetry and he stumbled up against a false quantity, or what he regarded as such. He at once got up and pitched the volume across the room in disgust, probably with an accompaniment of expressions not loud but deep. Regarding which behaviour, two remarks seem natural. The first is that possibly Buchanan was right and Porson wrong. At Eton, as is well known, Porson was a poor quantitarian, and fell behind in consequence. He may have made up his leeway afterwards, but not likely, and certainly his line of scholarship was not in the direction of Latin Prosody.

But suppose Buchanan were wrong, what then? Is Shakespeare to be flung into the corner because many of his lines will not scan? An indignant critic of the *Agamemnon* has discovered, what I believe is the fact, that in that play Æschylus has violated Dawes's canon. Yet everybody that can reads the *Agamemnon*. Dr. Johnson points out that Milton uses the hideous solecism *vapulandum*. Only think of it! And yet we read *Paradise Lost*. Perhaps Porson did too, knowing nothing of *vapulandum*! Johnson was no such stickler, for he read and enjoyed Milton, *vapulandum* notwithstanding. He had also the highest opinion of Buchanan, both as a Latinist and as 'a great poetical genius,' and his authority on such matters, being both poet and critic himself, is much greater than Porson's, great though the latter was in his own department of research. Hallam is inclined to qualify the almost universal admiration of Buchanan's poetry, but one begins to doubt Hallam's judgment in this matter when he finds him preferring Buchanan's *De Sphæra* to the rest of his poetry. The *Sphere* may contain exquisite isolated passages 'equal to Virgil,' as the enthusiastic Guy Patin maintained, but it is not properly a poem at all. It is really a versified and very lame defence of the exploded Ptolemaic Astronomy, totally destitute of the human interest which inspires so much else that Buchanan wrote. On his own field of history Hallam is more of an authority, and here his admiration of Buchanan is unstinted and unequivocal. He extols the 'perspicuity and power' of the *History of Scottish Affairs*, recognises the 'purity' of its diction, and affirms that few writings of the Latinists are 'more redolent of the antique air,' and is almost as emphatic in his eulogy as Dryden, when the latter says of Buchanan, 'our isle may justly boast in him a writer comparable to any of the moderns, and excelled by few of the ancients.' Froude might be cited to the same effect, but enough has been said to establish Buchanan's fame and power in the world of letters.

Of course, care must be taken to distinguish the precise character of Buchanan's scholarship. He was not a scholar in the sense that Casaubon, or Porson, or Liddell and Scott were scholars. That is to say, he was not a classical antiquarian, or philologist, or grammarian, although he knew antiquities and such philology as was going, and had refurbished or even made a grammar or two as he went along. But he used these simply as instruments to his main aim as a scholar, which was to write as good Latin as Virgil, or Livy, or Horace, or Tacitus. There is nothing absurd or impossible in such an aim. I have heard ardent Aberdonians maintain that the late Dr. Melvin of their city wrote better Latin than Cicero, and, apart from the matter, I am quite ready to believe it. That Buchanan as good as accomplished his purpose we have already seen.

And be it remembered that all this cultivation of a Latin style was not mere dilettante work on his part. He and one Sturm of Strasbourg, along with other Humanists, had formed the design of making Latin the vernacular of Europe, and actually believed that it would ultimately become such. Hence they had a twofold purpose in writing Latin. They desired to forward this reform of a universal language, and they wished to be intelligible to a Latin-speaking posterity. I state this on the authority of Dr. P. Hume Brown, the well-known author of *George Buchanan, Humanist and Reformer*, and I should not advise any one rashly to contradict Dr. Brown on any Buchanan matter. He seems to me to have mastered the entire subject, and to have left very little for subsequent research to do, unless some lucky 'find' of new sources should occur. I have been able to glean nothing from any quarter that I have not found already known to Dr. Brown, and recorded by him, unless it be some such small fact as the presence of Joseph Scaliger in Edinburgh in 1566, along with his friend Chastaigner, but not expressly to see Buchanan; and other little things of that sort. I do not pretend to contribute any fresh Buchanan materials. My object is the humble, but not, I hope, useless one of boiling down Dr. Brown and the other scientific biographers, and attempting a brief popular presentation of what Buchanan was and did.

Another proof of the varied power of Buchanan is found in the storm he raised as a controversialist, in the still burning question as to the guilt or innocence of Mary Queen of Scots. In 1571, four years after the Scottish people had deposed their sovereign, Buchanan published a pamphlet, or what in these days would probably have taken the shape of a magazine article, with the title *Detectio Mariæ Reginæ*, i.e. *The Detection or Exposure of Queen Mary*, or as an editor of to-day would have been sure to head it, *The Truth about the Queen*. Buchanan's object in this publication is to vindicate the Scottish people and their leaders before the public opinion of Europe for having, after the murder of Darnley, brought Mary's career as sovereign to a close, as being not only a public danger, but a public scandal. That the vigour of the *brochure* itself, backed up by Buchanan's immense reputation, went far to make Mary an impossible factor in European politics, is beyond question. To the same extent he made himself the *bête noire* of Mary's friends and apologists, and very brutal and very black they certainly made him out to be. In more recent times a school of sentimental historians has arisen, who refuse to see in Mary either fault or flaw, and recognise in her a sort of spotless goddess, of irresistible charm, thrown away upon an unworthy age. Not content with pity—it would be inhuman not to feel it in any case— they show how true it is that pity is akin to love, and falling victims in some degree to the spell which ruined the unhappy and love-maddened Chastelard, they conduct a necessarily Platonic flirtation with their idol's romantic and fascinating memory, across the separating interval of three hundred years. Had Mary been ugly, or even plain, she would have had fewer champions.

In vituperation of Buchanan they are not a whit behind his contemporary assailants. Mr. Hosack, for instance, one of the most ingenious of Mary's modern defenders, calmly says, 'Buchanan was without doubt the most venal and unscrupulous of men.' His usual way of alluding to the *Detectio* is 'Buchanan's famous libel,' varied occasionally by 'the highly coloured narrative of Buchanan,' or 'the subsequently invented slanders of Buchanan,' or 'the slanderous narrative of Buchanan,' or 'the atrocious libel of Buchanan.' Sir John Skelton, whose treatment of the subject is distinguished by a literary grace which cannot be claimed for Mr. Hosack, is on a level with him when he reaches Buchanan. 'Buchanan's atrocious libel' is common form with the Marians, and Sir John has it. Perhaps his gentlest reference is when he speaks of 'the industrious animosity of the man who had been her pensioner,' and when he desires to be specially severe, he speaks of 'grotesque adventures invented, or at least adapted, by Buchanan, whose virulent animosities were utterly unscrupulous, and whose clumsy invective was as bitter as it was pedantic.' The present is not the place to inquire into the truth or falsehood of these statements. They are adduced merely as a tribute to Buchanan's power. 'Woe unto you when all men shall speak well of you,' does not logically justify the counter statement, 'Good for you when all men shall speak ill of you'; but when a controversialist has been abused by his opponents as Buchanan has been, it is at least a proof that he has been found a formidable antagonist, either for his ability or veracity, or both, and that in the direct ratio of the violence with which they attack him.

One other aspect of Buchanan's varied power seems to call for some mention. Up to the middle of this century, a chapbook usually entitled *The Witty and Entertaining Exploits of George Buchanan*, sometimes adding *The King's Jester*, ran through many editions original and revised, and had a certain vogue all over Scotland among a considerable class—not the most refined, certainly—of the population. It is an ignorant, coarse, and indecent production, and can be read only by the historical student for the purpose of investigating the popular taste of its time. Its description of Buchanan as the 'Fule' instead of the tutor of King James, and its placing him at the English court of James, who did not ascend the throne of England until Buchanan had been twenty-one years dead, are sufficient commentary on its historical accuracy. At first sight one might imagine that it had been put together by an enemy of Buchanan, but its brutish zeal in holding up Buchanan as a desperately clever fellow who was continually turning the tables and raising the laugh against people who wished to take him off, and who were generally English, and often English nobles, bishops or other clergy, show that it was earnest in its admiration according to its dim and dirty lights.

Buchanan was a humorist, and saw the ludicrous side of existence with a depth and keenness and enjoyment very different from the barbarian faculty which produced the 'merry bourds' of Knox and certain of his iconoclastic cronies. Even the prospect of having soon to leave the world could not make him utterly solemn, although the circumstances lend a grim aspect to the humour which may make it distasteful to wooden seriousness. 'Tell the people who sent you,' he said to the macer of the Court of Session, who came to summon him for something objectionable in some of his writings, 'tell them I am summoned before a higher tribunal.' When good John Davidson called on him and reminded him of the usual evangelical consolations, he repaid him with some original causticity *à propos* of the Romish doctrine of the Mass, which would no doubt delight that worthy man. He never had much money at any time, and less than usual at the close; and when, on counting it up with his attendant, he found that there was not enough to bury him, he directed it to be given to the poor. But 'what about the funeral?' naturally asked the servitor. 'Well,' Buchanan said, 'he was very indifferent about that,' as he meditated on the dilemma in which he saw he was placing the people of Edinburgh, who had not been over kind to the greatest scholar of the age. 'If they will not bury me,' he said, 'they can let me lie where I am, or throw my body where they like.' Of course, as he knew, they had to bury him, so he could enjoy his posthumous triumph of wit; but they had their repartee, denying him a gravestone for a generation or two.

There is a weird humour in the famous interview between himself on the one hand and the Melvilles, Andrew and James, on the other, who had crossed from St. Andrews to Edinburgh to see him shortly before he passed away. They found him teaching his young attendant his *a b, ab*. Andrew Melville, amused by the spectacle of the greatest scholar in Europe engaged in so disproportionate a task, made a suitable observation. 'Better this than stealing sheep,' quoth Buchanan, or 'than being idill,' he added, which latter he maintained to be as bad as the stealing of sheep. Then the conversation wandered to his *History*, which was by this time in the hands of the printer. The Melvilles noticed in the proofs the well-known and ugly story of Mary's having got Rizzio's body removed to the tomb of James V. They suggested that the king might take offence at this reflection on his mother's memory, and that the publication might be stopped. 'Tell me,' said the dying historian, 'if it is true.' They said they thought so. 'Then I will bide his feud, and all his kin's,' was the answer. There was, no doubt, a dash of the heroic in this, but there was a chuckle in it too, as the speaker reflected that the king who had neglected him, and whom he had flogged for persistent boyish insolence, according to the pedagogic fashion of the time, would once more have his pride humbled at his hands when he was gone.

No story was better known in Scotland than his correction of the king, and his now unrepeatable sarcasm in reply to the Countess of Mar's haughty demand how he, a mere man of learning, could dare to lift his hand upon the Lord's anointed. It tickled the popular mind, and along with other reports of Buchanan's fun—for it is not to be supposed that his table-talk with the Scaligers, or even with Knox, was wholly funereal in character—indeed we know it was not—formed a sort of Buchanan myth, to which every witling who thought he had invented a good thing, and wanted to get it listened to by fathering it on a well-known name—a device not yet extinct—would contribute further bulk, although not more ornament. In this way an idea of Buchanan as a man of mirth and facetiousness[1] would take root and spread in the public consciousness, and as the people could not get at the real Buchanan for his Latin, they formed a picture of him according to their own uncivilised conceptions. Hence the chapbooks—a hideous reflection from a cracked and distorted mirror, but still showing that there was something to reflect.

Such was Buchanan, political thinker, practical statesman, poet, scholar, historian, controversialist, humorist, and great in all these diverse directions—certainly a personality worth knowing in greater detail.

CHAPTER II
CHARACTERISTICS

Buchanan's life, like the lives of most people who have done anything worth speaking of in their time, divides itself roughly into two sections—the period of preparation, and the period of performance. What I shall call his period of performance, or at all events chief performance, was from the time when he finally returned to Scotland, after an absence abroad, with brief interruptions, of twenty-two years, and spent the remaining twenty-one years of his life in more or less intimate occupation with the public affairs of his country. On the 19th of August 1561, Queen Mary, then in her nineteenth year, landed at Leith, and was escorted to Holyrood by her enthusiastic subjects, by whom she was also serenaded at night in a style which, as the queen's French retinue thought, showed more heart than art. Shortly before or after this date, Buchanan, now fifty-five years old, also appeared in Scotland, for his final settlement there. It is a curious coincidence that these two persons, eminent alike in their widely divergent spheres, and destined alternately to a literary friendship that was pleasant to both, and a political antagonism that was fatal to one of them, should have appeared on the scene of their sympathies and conflicts practically at the same time. I have said that the division of Buchanan's life into a period of preparation and a period of performance is a rough division. By that I mean that what really deserves to be called performance could not be absolutely excluded from the preparation period, and that, to some extent, one stage of the performance period was often a preparation for the next; but taken with this qualification, the division is a sufficiently valid one.

It was, for instance, mainly during the preparation or foreign period that Buchanan wrote those poems which stamped him not only as a man of wit and poetic genius, but as the first Latin stylist in Europe of his day. During this period, too, he acquired from classic and other sources those broad and comprehensive ideas on the leading questions of the day which made him the thinker and Humanist as contrasted with the mere cleric or scholastic obscurantist. It was then also that, through observation on the spot, he was able to comprehend the 'true inwardness' of the struggle that was going forward between the old order of things and the new, and often give practical advice that was useful. In this period, too, he completed that thorough study of the Roman and Protestant controversy which ended in determining him to identify himself publicly with the Protestant side in the great conflict that was on foot—in itself no inconsiderable event. All this was undoubtedly performance of no mean order, but from the Scottish national point of view, and from the point of view of general history, on which the special Scottish history exerted so profound an influence, it was preparatory to the great work he did in his native land. His Latin and his various Continental activities are forgotten, but his Scottish work is still memorable. Yet it was because he was the great Humanist and unequalled Latinist, as well as the thinker and experienced observer of affairs, that he was able to command the ear of learned and diplomatic Europe, and through them to make the events that were happening in his country a factor in the world's history. His foreign performance was therefore, in reality, a preparation for his crowning performance at home. I shall not labour the point of one stage of his performance being preparatory to another.

Of course I do not mean to say that Buchanan did all this consciously and systematically; that he deliberately prepared abroad, and then came and deliberately performed at home. Few men, especially men of Buchanan's type, shape their lives on such lines of exact and exhaustive purpose. I leave out of account the unhappily large class who foolishly, and even wickedly, throw away their lives, and have hardly ever tried or desired to make a better of it. I confine myself to those who do get something out of life for themselves or society, or both. But I doubt if any, beyond a small minority even of this class, begin life with a distinct aim at reaching what they end life by becoming. There is, of course, the famous case of Whittington, who set himself in cold blood to become Lord Mayor of London. But for one Whittington there have been centuries of Lord Mayors who never dreamt of the Mansion House when they started business in the City. The glory and the turtle came upon them, virtually unsolicited; and even Whittington would probably not have addressed himself as he did to his high achievement, had it not been for the unique campanula of inspiration caught by his ear alone. Probably Napoleon early laid his plans for attaining the mastership of France, possibly of Europe; but did Cæsar begin life with a determination to conquer Rome and become its dictator, or Cromwell with a sketch-plan for cutting off his king's head, cashiering his country's parliament, and making himself Lord Protector and military despot?

Millionaires are seldom so of set design. They begin, most probably, by aiming at a competent fortune, but having got that length, the acquired delight in pulling the strings of an extensive and possibly adventurous undertaking, and not mere miserly greed, has kept them at a task which they find they can perform, until the millions roll in as a justification of their ideas and processes. In politics and the professions men probably set out with a general aim at the best position and the most money they can make for themselves; but very few, I should imagine, of those who have reached the greatest eminence or prosperity possible to them said in their youth, 'I mean to be Prime Minister, or Lord Chancellor, or Archbishop of Canterbury, or President of the Royal College of Physicians, or of the Royal Academy.' Buchanan seems to have belonged to a type of character which does not include either of the classes of persons just considered. Neither cupidity nor ambition nor any of the ordinary self-aggrandising motives seems to have had much, if any, place in his character. Apostrophising Buchanan in his Funeral Elegy, Joseph Scaliger says:—

> 'Contemptis opibus, spretis popularibus auris,
> Ventosæque fugax ambitionis, obis.'

> 'Despising wealth, spurning the mob's applause, and
> shunning vain ambition, thou passest away.'

This was literally true. Buchanan lived from hand to mouth during the greater part of his career. But there is no evidence that he ever tried to make a fortune. He might have prospered in the Church, as Dunbar was willing to do. But he had ideas of his own on that subject, and neither gold nor dignities could tempt him to sell his soul.

Begging Letter-Writer

He was often 'hard up,' but it does not appear to have depressed his spirits. Indeed, he is never sprightlier, more epigrammatically witty, or more genially humorous than when he is what some of us might call 'begging' from some wealthy friend who could appreciate his genius and accomplishments. Here, for instance, is a 'begging letter' to Queen Mary, in the days when they were still friends, and read Livy, and doubtless indulged in fencing-matches of wit together:—

> 'Do quod adest: opto quod abest tibi: dona darentur
> Aurea, sors animo si foret æqua meo.
> Hoc leve si credis, paribus me ulciscere donis:
> Et quod abest, opta tu mihi: da quod adest.'

Which may be literally, or nearly so, according 'to the best of my knowledge and belief,' as the affidavits say:—

> 'To you I give what I do have: for you I wish what you
> don't have:
> Golden, indeed, would be my gifts, were Fortune equal to

my will.
If you should chance to think this levity, in equal levities
have your revenge:
For me wish you what I don't have: to me give you what
you do have.'

Dr. Hume Brown puts it neatly into rhyme thus:—

'I give you what I have: I wish you what you lack:
And weightier were my gift, were fortune at my back.
Perchance you think I jest? A like jest then I crave:
Wish for me what I lack, and give me what you have.'

Take another in the same strain:—

'Ad Jacobum, Moraviæ Comitem.
'Si magis est, ut Christus ait, donare beatum,
Quam de munifica dona referre manu:
Aspice quam faveam tibi: sis ut dando beatus,
Non renuo fieri, te tribuente, miser.'

'To James, Earl of Moray.

'If, as Christ says, it is more blessed to give than to receive
gifts from a munificent hand, just see what a favour I am
doing you: that you may be blessed in giving, I am ready to
play miserable receiver to your happy donor.'

Or, to cite Dr. Brown again:—

'It is more blest, saith Holy Writ, to give than to receive:
How great, then, is your debt to me, who take whate'er you
give!'

With equally humorous familiarity he sends in an application, 'Ad
Matthæum Leviniæ Comitem, Scotiæ Proregem' (To Matthew, Earl of
Lennox, Regent of Scotland'). I quote only the concluding couplet:—

'Denique da quidvis, podagram modo deprecor unam:
Munus erit medicis aptius illa suis.'

That is—

'To be brief, give me whatever you like—only, not your gout.
That will be a more appropriate fee for the doctors who are
trying to cure it.'

Or to fall back on Dr. Brown's translation once more:—

'Since I am poor and you are rich, what happy chance is thine!
My modest wishes, too, you know — one nugget from your mine!
Only, whatever be your gift, let it not be your gout:
That, a meet present for your leech, I'd rather go without.'

These are merely samples of many communications, similar in object and style, which he addressed, at various periods of his life, to quarters where he thought they would not be ill-taken. As a rule, he supported himself by 'regenting' in colleges, or acting as tutor in royal or noble families. It was only when he could not make a better of it that he asked Society, through its most likely magnates, to give him something 'to go on with.' What else could he do? Carlyle's description of Thackeray as 'writing for his life' could never have applied to Buchanan. Literature was not yet a profession or 'bread-study.' It was not till next century that Milton got £5 for *Paradise Lost*; and even Shakespeare made his money less as a writer than as a showman. The idea of Buchanan or Erasmus — a much more importunate beggar than Buchanan — going into business, say the wine or the wool trade, would have been absurd. They would have ruined any house that adopted them in two or three years, to say nothing of the indecency of allowing intellectual leaders of high genius to be lost in work which could be much better done by humbler men. There was nothing else for it, in Buchanan's case, but to do as he did.

Of course, in this age of contract and commerce, we are apt to associate an idea of meanness and pitifulness with the conduct of Buchanan and Erasmus and others in this matter. Our first feeling is that nobody should give any other body anything except according to bargain. Every man should be independent, and if he asks anything outside a contract, he might as well go bankrupt at once. He must clearly be a weakling, and the weak must go to the wall. The feudal sentiment, however, amidst which Buchanan lived, was entirely different, and had a nobler side than ours, although one does not want feudalism back merely on that account. Kings and lords took everything to themselves, in the shape of power and possession, that they could lay their hands on; but it was on the understanding that they were to make a generous use of what they had appropriated. *Noblesse oblige* was still a maxim with vitality in it. The right men acknowledged it, and acted on it; the ruffians, as their manner is, wherever they are placed in life, ignored it. Patronage was not an act of grace: it was a duty. It was part of the honourable service to society, by which the patron's tenure of his prosperity was conditioned. More particularly must this duty have been recognised by right-minded possessors of power and wealth who had felt the influence of the Renaissance, that mighty and far-reaching effort of the human intellect to assert its freedom and its varied energies against the narrowing and obscurantist influences of scholasticism, reduced to its then existing state of enslavement, often against its better knowledge and attempts at self-emancipation, by Ecclesiastical authority, wielding the weapon of Papal and Conciliar decree, sanctioned by fire and faggot.

Then there was still the tradition of hospitality which the Old Church, with all its faults, had kept up. In these contractual days of ours, there is very little hospitality, as it was defined by the Author of Christianity. A modern dinner is generally a meeting of creditors, or a combination of clever or stupid epicureans, the better to amuse or otherwise enjoy themselves, according to their tastes in meat and drink, or even conversation. It is often a case of undisguised 'treating' on the part of the so-called host, who wants to use his so-called guests for a purpose, and whose performance might very appropriately go into a schedule to some of the Bribery and Corruption Acts. But in the days of the Old Church, a wandering or needy scholar would have been welcomed at many, if not all, of the religious houses, and treated on a very different footing from our applicants for relief at the casual wards of one of our workhouses, probably the only institution resembling Christian hospitality authorised by modern organised society.

This latter may be a better arrangement, for anything I know to the contrary. All I say is that it is different from what was recognised in Buchanan's day. It would never occur to Buchanan that he was doing anything inconsistent with self-respect in putting his position before people like Queen Mary, or Moray, or Lennox, and asking their temporary aid or a permanent office. They had taken over the wealth of the religious houses; did not their hospitalities pass with it? They had divided up the country among themselves and others; were they not honourably bound to see that a great civilising force like Buchanan was not extinguished? Besides, he understood his own value. A man is not six feet six inches high without being aware of it. He knew what he was, and what he had made himself, and what he was worth, and that he was giving as good as he was getting, or likely to get. In those days a great master of the New Learning was an object of the highest admiration, as a sort of intellectual Magician. Moreover, he was a power, in as far as he was a leader of contemporary thought and learning.

In these respects Buchanan was an invaluable acquisition to persons like Mary, or Moray, or Lennox, or Knox, who must have winked at a good deal in Buchanan, which he would not have stood in a less potent ally. In his prime, and even until his death, no one had an equal command over the universal ear of cultured Europe. To the rulers of his time he was worth what, say, fifty friendly editors of newspapers—including the *Times* and all the sixpenny weeklies, as far as they are worth anything would be to a politician of to-day. To Queen Mary especially, with her refined intellectual tastes and her ambition to be a figure in the world, it was no small matter to have the greatest and most brilliant scholar-poet of the day as a part of her court, whether he read Livy and exchanged wit with herself, or officiated as her poet-laureate on great occasions. As a mere ornament he was worth a considerable fraction of her best diamond necklace.

I am dwelling on this point because it will save time and trouble afterwards, and accordingly I ask further if Edie Ochiltree, in later times, and in a less feudalistic state of public sentiment, could beg round the district, without loss of respect, on the strength of his badge and uniform, testifying to past good service in his time and station, why should not an eminent public servant like Buchanan, in a totally different state of general feeling on such matters, ask society, through representatives of it who, he knew, should not and would not treat him roughly, to help him in prosecuting his shining and useful career? He had done a good work on the High Street of the World. He had sung it a song or played it a melody such as it would hear nowhere else. Was he not entitled to send round his hat among the listeners? Is it not what is done by every book-writer of to-day, who, when the last page is finished, sends out a confederate in the shape of a publisher to canvass the public—for a consideration—with the book in one hand and the hat in the other? Is it not what is done, *inter alia*, by every Parliamentary lawyer, who goes into the House of Commons to grind his axe, when the fitting occasion arises, and he says to his party leader, 'I have fought two general elections for you. I have spoken for you unnumbered times in the House and on the platform. I have voted for you, up hill and down dale, through thick and thin, right or wrong, and now I will trouble you for that Chancellorship, or that Chief-Justiceship, or that Attorney-Generalship, or that Puisne or County Court Judgeship that has just fallen vacant'? Except that Buchanan and his work were not shams, but realities, the cases are the same.

Buchanan's enemies say that in accepting maintenance or preferment he sold his independence to the donors, and when it is answered that he showed anything but want of independence in the case of Queen Mary and others, whom he subsequently came to oppose in the public interest, they tack about and accuse him of the basest ingratitude—in biting the hand that fed him, as they put it. It is as if in these days Sir Gorgias Midas, M.P., were to say to some editor who had noticed a speech of his unfavourably, 'Ungrateful scribbler, have I not, over and over again, dined you and wined you with the best that larder and cellar can produce, and do you now turn and rend me?' There have been editors who would have answered, 'Presumptuous moneybag, I suppose I paid fully for my dinner with my company, and I am perfectly free to criticise you as you deserve.' Buchanan stood equally free in his relations to his patrons. From the personal point of view, whether his connection were regarded as an ornament, a pleasure, or a utility, his alliance was worth his subsidy. From the public point of view it was their duty, as trustees for the public property and progress, to maintain a great civiliser like Buchanan in a position where his powers had scope, while it was Buchanan's privilege and duty to exercise his creative and critical capacities in the public interest without fear or favour. And this, as will be seen, is what Buchanan substantially did. Knox and Melville repeatedly reminded Queen Mary and King James that there was another kingdom in the realm besides theirs—the kingdom of Christ, to wit—and suggested, or rather demanded, that their Majesties should not meddle with officials of this spiritual kingdom like themselves, the said Knox and Melville. This claim they rested on a supernatural, and therefore disputable, basis. But there could be nothing disputable about the ground Buchanan stood on. He too was a potentate—of the intellect; a king of thought, learning, and poetic might, and in that dominion, when it was necessary, bore himself with a courage and independence that have not always been successfully reproduced by his successors, when confronted with the monarchies and lordships of material power and glory.

No Notoriety Hunter

This discussion arose in our endeavour to determine Buchanan's character so far as money-making was concerned. He was no money-maker. *Contemptis opibus*—'despising wealth'—is, as we have seen, Joseph Scaliger's account of him, meaning thereby that personally he did not care for more money than would maintain the much other than money-making career which he liked, and had set his heart on, keeping himself independent by the labour of a scholar, but not hesitating to ask payment, when he wanted it, from a society that was morally indebted to him. His indifference, however, to wealth as a life-object must not be confounded with the counsel of the ascetic preacher who urges his hearers to forget the present world in thoughts of the world to come, and wins, perhaps, a better living by an eloquent and pessimistic sermon on the text which says that 'the love of money is the root of all evil.' There is nothing to show that Buchanan did not hold, with all sensible people, that there is a sense in which the love of money is the root of all good, inasmuch as it is the men of strong cupidity who organise industry and commerce, thereby laying that foundation of material wealth without which there can be no superstructure of leisured thought, learning, or art, acting, it may be, only as the dray-horses of civilisation—some of them, of course, are a good deal more—but worthy of all the corn they consume, although were one desirous of exchanging ideas, it would not be to their sumptuous stables that he would resort.

Neither does he appear to have set his heart upon the ordinary objects of ambition, in the shape of fame or power. 'Dear is fame to the rhyming tribe.' 'That dearest wish of every poetic bosom—to be distinguished,' said Burns in his preface to the first edition of his poems, and he, if any one, was entitled to speak. But in the same preface he also says that to amuse himself amidst toil, to transcribe the feelings in his own breast, to find some counterpoise to the struggles of a world alien and uncouth to the poetic mind—'these were his motives for courting the Muses, and in these he found Poetry to be its own reward.' In other words, the poet may desire fame and distinction for what he has done, yet it need not have been the desire of fame and distinction that made him do it. Buchanan seems to have been even more self-controlled or more indifferent than this account of matters might imply. His numerous efforts had won him the highest reputation, but he had taken no pains to advertise himself. He had handed his productions here and there to friends who wished to see them, and it was only the solicitation of those friends that prevented his consigning to everlasting obscurity some of the brightest things he, or indeed any one else, ever wrote.

His most famous production as a poet, his version of the Hebrew Psalms, or rather series of poems based upon these, was certainly not written for fame. Every Humanist of eminence was expected to try his hand upon the Psalms, and when Buchanan found himself in Portugal under lock and key, at the instance of the Inquisition, among a set of monks, whom he hits off as equally good-natured and ignorant, and who had been told off to instruct him in orthodoxy, he addressed himself to a classic rendering of the Psalms with the double purpose of discharging his duty by his Humanistic Vocation, and doing something that might redeem his time and his temper from the boredom of the uncongenial society amidst which misfortune had placed him. There does not seem in all this much of that passionate desire of distinction to which Burns confesses. It is said, however, that fame was his object in commencing and carrying on his poem on the *Sphere*, which was undoubtedly planned on an elaborate and extensive scale. If fame was his desire, it was not a very consuming one, for he was five-and-twenty years at least over it, and left it unfinished at last, although goaded by friends to hasten its production.

What does he say on the matter himself? Writing to Tycho Brahe in 1576, six years before his death, and more than twenty after he began to work at the *Sphere*, he says that bad health had compelled him, *spem scribendi carminis in posterum penitus abjicere,*—'completely to abandon the hope of writing a poem for posterity.' Three years afterwards, writing to a literary friend in England, who, like many others, kept dunning him for his promised books, and even for 'copy,' he says, with respect to his 'astronomical' aims in poetry, he had not so much voluntarily abandoned them, as been obliged reluctantly to submit to the deprivation of them; *neque enim aut nunc libet nugari, aut si maxime vellem per ætatem licet. Accessit eo historiæ scribendæ labor,*—'for neither am I now greatly disposed for mere trifling, nor, were I never so much disposed, will my years allow it. Then in addition to my other difficulties there is the labour of writing my *History*'; the plain meaning being that as his years forbade him to do both the *History* and the *Sphere*, he elected to go on with the *History* and give up the *Sphere*, as a form of *nugari* or 'dilettantism.'

All this does not look very like a burning eagerness for posthumous fame, at all events of the kind that moves a certain class of people to leave money for hospitals, or almshouses, or learned foundations, to perpetuate names that would otherwise never have risen out of obscurity or escaped oblivion. As a matter of fact, Buchanan knew that he was celebrated, but no one had a poorer opinion of the work that had won him reputation than he had himself, not from the modesty of merit, as the common form carelessly puts it, but from the consciousness of merit, and because he felt that it was in him to do better. He hated the idea of having more celebrity than he deserved, and wanted to produce something that would show he was not an impostor or a quack. In short, he did not want more fame, but what he thought a better and honester title to the fame he had. That, however, is not the passion for fame, but simply self-respect, and an unselfish anxiety for the good name of those friends who had staked their reputation for taste and judgment on his ability for turning out the highest class of work. This is not the love of glory, but something better, although even if it were, it would not necessarily be either weak or wrong, provided the subject of it knew what he was doing in giving a rational scope to a natural impulse, and that he could and would give humanity something worth the prize of its praise.

Buchanan himself tells us why he gave up the *Sphere* and took up the *History*. It was primarily to gratify his friends, who thought that such a work was a want of the time, more useful and more suitable to Buchanan's years than poetry; while he himself assures us, and there is no reason to doubt his declaration, that he desired to set before his royal pupil, James VI., the warnings and the encouragements derivable from the story of his predecessors on the throne, including his own ill-advised and ill-fated mother. It was no fault of Buchanan's if James despised his teacher's counsel, and, listening to flatterers, took up with the Divine Right doctrine, by impressing which on his unhappy son, both through precept and example, he virtually destined him to jump the life to come from the scaffold of Whitehall.

Buchanan's friends seem to have tried to tempt him to undertake the *History* by representing that no subject was *aut uberius ad laudem, aut firmius ad memoriæ conservandam diuturnitatem,*—'better fitted to win him renown or prolong his memory.' It is not on the strength of such hopes, however, that he describes himself as working. It was, by his own account, only the shame of leaving unfinished a task he had engaged himself to his friends to perform that made him persevere at a labour which, he says, *in ætate integra permolestus, nunc vero in hac meditatione mortis, inter mortalitatis metum, et desinendi pudorem, non potest non lentus esse et ingratus, quando nec cessare licet, nec progredi lubet,*—'would, even in the flower of my age, have been a burden, but now, in contemplation of my end, what between the dread of death interrupting me before I am done, and the shame there would be in abandoning my undertaking, I neither find myself free to stop, nor feel any pleasure in going on.' Not much there of glory for himself, although something of an heroic devotion to the claims of friendship and the call of duty!

CHAPTER III
CHARACTERISTICS—(*continued*)

Did not seek power

Scaliger's ascription to Buchanan of a spirit superior to the temptations of wealth and fame seems thus fairly well justified; but what of his further claim that he was insensible to ambition? He rose to be the foremost Latin poet and man of letters, or indeed poet and man of letters of any kind in his day, and to the highest positions, political, ecclesiastical, educational, in his native land. Did he reach all this without aiming at it? Did it all come upon him unsolicited? Substantially, it would seem, that was so. The key to his plan of life, I believe, is to be found in the beginning of the short autobiography which he wrote (1580) in the third person, two years before his death, not from motives of egotism, but at the request of friends. He is stating how he came to be sent to the University of Paris when about fourteen, and then he says, *ibi cum studiis literarum, maxime carminibus scribendis, operam dedisset, partim naturæ impulsu, partim necessitate (quod hoc unum studiorum genus adolescentiæ proponebatur)*, etc.,—'devoting himself there to literary studies, and chiefly to writing verses, partly from natural impulse and partly from necessity, that being the only sort of study open to youthful learners.'

That is really Buchanan in a nutshell. He followed the bent of his genius, and did not pick and choose his work, but performed, to the best of his ability, the task placed before him by Destiny. He lived up to his nature and his Fate, did with his might what his hand found to do, then took up the next undertaking that came along, and handled it in the same fashion. He waited upon 'time and the hour' rather than sought to force its hand—a very good way, if not indeed the best way, to confront life and its problems, for those who are wise enough and strong enough to do it. He made himself master of the spirit, ideas, and style of the great writers and thinkers of classic antiquity, because it was the work that lay nearest to his hand, and because he liked it—passionately—and could not rest until it was all and easily his own, and not because he thought he could make it pay, whether in money or reputation, or both. Except in the case of the unlucky and unfinished *Sphere*, he did not sit down to compose poetry deliberately and in cold blood, at the rate of so many scores or hundreds of lines before breakfast or dinner, as certain 'poets' are said to have done, or do. His best work of this kind was struck out of him like the fire from the flint, by the demand of the occasion, or the suggestion of friends, or an inspiration or impulse that came upon him at the moment.

It was the request of James V. (1537) that led to his becoming the most powerful satirist of his time and country, much above Lyndsay, at least on a level with Dunbar, and second only to Burns. His 'Psalms' were written (1550-51) to kill time while imprisoned in a Portuguese monastery. His Elegies, Epigrams, Tragedies, Masques, Addresses (1530-66) were thrown off in answer to the call of the moment and the circumstances. The *Detectio Reginæ* (1569-71) was composed at the desire of the great anti-despotic and reforming party to which he belonged. The 'Admonition to the Trew Lordis' and the 'Chameleon' were political tracts for the times designed to stimulate the flagging zeal of the friends of freedom. The *De Jure* (1570-79) was inspired by a present and a foreseen necessity of making Liberty impregnable as against the reactionaries of Absolutism. The *History* was undertaken and completed (1569-82) less for a scientific than for a patriotic and politico-paideutic purpose, to set his country and its constitution in a true light before the world, and to help in moulding its future king into the constitutional ruler of a free people.

He held many appointments, and executed many commissions, not a few of them of the highest responsibility and dignity, but most of them sought him, not he them. Lord Cassilis had him for tutor-companion (1532-37). King James V. engaged him as tutor for one of his children (1538-39). The King of Portugal employed him to aid in founding and conducting his College at Coimbra, and did his best, though in vain, to retain him in his kingdom (1547-52). The famous Maréchal de Brissac chose him to mould the mind of his son, and sometimes had him at a Council of War (1555-60). Queen Mary attached him to her Court, and as we have seen, read Livy with him, and, no doubt, much else (1562). The General Assembly of the Reformed Church of Scotland chose him, though a layman, as their Moderator (1567), he having already sat four years as a member and aided them in drawing up their *First Book of Discipline*. He was appointed by Regent Moray Principal of St. Leonard's College, St. Andrews (1566), to reorganise its curriculum and constitution. He was selected as Secretary to the Commission sent by the Scots Government to deal with the high questions at issue between Queens Elizabeth and Mary (1568-69). The Scots Parliament chose him to the extremely responsible office of Tutor to the youthful King James VI. (1570), and continued him in that position nominally until his death (1582). He sat as a member of the Scots Parliament (1570-78) in virtue of his keepership of the Privy Seal, and did secretarial work for it, which nobody else was qualified to do, while at the same time assisting the General Assembly in revising their Book of 'Policy.' This keepership he may have solicited—he subsequently resigned it—although there is no proof of that, but all the other appointments came to him, and engaged his best ability as they passed him in procession.

Sir James Melville backs Scaliger

This view of Buchanan's character and scheme of life is confirmed by the remarkable and elaborate account of him given, in his own *Memoirs*, by Sir James Melville of Halhill (1545-1617), a professional courtier and diplomatist who had served on the Continent in important missions and affairs, and had been a confidential servant both to Queen Mary and her son James VI. He is describing the guardians of the boy-king at Stirling (1570-78), and after having highly eulogised the Governor, he proceeds: 'The Laird of Dromwhassel, his Maiestie's maister of houshald, was ambitious and greedy, and had gretest cair how till advance himself and his friendis. The twa abbots [Cambuskenneth and Dryburgh] were wyse and modest; my Lady Mar was wyse and schairp, and held [*i.e.* kept] the King in great aw; and sa did Mester George Buchwhennen. Mester Peter Young[2] was gentiller, and was laith till offend the King at any tym, and used himself wairily, as a man that had mynd of his awin weill, be keeping of his Maiestie's favour. Bot Mester George was a stoik philosopher, and looked not far before the hand; a man of notable qualities for his learning and knawledge in Latin poesie, mekle maid accompt of in other contrees, plaisant in company, rehersing at all occasions moralities short and fecfull, whereof he had aboundance, and invented wher he wanted.

'He was also of gud religion for a poet, bot he was easily abused, and sa facill that he was led with any company that he hanted for the tyme, quhilk maid him factious in his auld dayes; for he spak and wret as they that wer about him for the tym infourmed him. For he was become sleperie and cairles, and followed in many thingis the vulgair oppinion, for he was naturally populaire, and extrem vengeable against any man that had offendit him, quhilk was his gretest fault. For he wret dispytfull invectives against the Erle of Monteith, for some particulaires that was between him and the Laird of Buchwhennen; and became the Erle of Morton's gret ennemy, for ane hackney of his that chancit to be tane fra his saru[v]and during the civil troubles, and was bocht be the Regent; wha had na will to part with the said horse, he was sa sur of foot and sa easy, that albeit Mester George had oft tymes requyred him again, he culd not get him, and wher he had bene the

Regentis gret frend of before, he becam his deadly ennemy, and spak evil of him fra that tym fourth in all places and at all occasions. Dromwhassel also, because the Regent kepit all the casualtes[3] to himself, and wald let nathing fall till v[u]thers that wer about the King, becam also his ennemy, and sa did they all that wer about his Maiestie.'

Melville was scarcely the man to take the measure of Buchanan on the more important side of his character, but he may be trusted to have given an honest view of him according to his lights—which, in some serious respects, were darkness—as well as of the impression which Buchanan had made on better judges of remarkable men than was the worthy Sir James himself. The latter's preface is a charming piece of *naïveté*. He tells us that though a courtier he had dealt faithfully and not flatteringly with 'princes,' but had not found it a paying procedure, and hints that if he had it to do over again, he might sail on the opposite tack. He had advised the Laird of Carmichael to do so, who profited greatly by the advice, both for himself and his friends, but did not show much gratitude to his counsellor, as the latter complains— rather unreasonably, one would say, since, if you corrupt a man's *morale*, you must not be disappointed if he treats you accordingly. Perhaps Sir James recovers his honest standing by the honest simplicity with which he confesses his leanings to dishonesty, like the M. de Bussy whom he quotes as also bewailing, too late, the honesty of his courtier career, but excusing himself on the ground that he could not help it, as it was his 'nature to.'

All the more trustworthy, however, is probably the distinction Sir James draws between Peter Young and Buchanan. 'Mester Peter' was evidently no Nathanael in his critic's view, and his subsequent good fortune, as attested by history, shows that his character had been accurately enough diagnosed. There is no reason to doubt, accordingly, that Sir James is equally correct in describing Buchanan as one who 'looked not far before the hand.' That is, he was not a calculating person, and set his duties above his interests; did his work to the best of his ability, and took his reward if, as, and when it came, but was really less anxious about securing the reward than about doing the work as it ought to be done.

A Faithful Mentor

His whole connection with James makes this plain. It begins with his *Genethliacon* or Birthday Ode, in which, after apostrophising the infant prince as the hope of all who desired the unity and consequent tranquillity of the two kingdoms, he addresses the *felices felici prole parentes* ('parents to be felicitated on an offspring born to a felicitous career'), and under guise of a sketch, in verse of Virgilian elevation and beauty, of the standard of character up to which they should train their child, lays down with 'faithful' outspokenness the lines of duty on which their own lives should run, and warns them of the ruin which neglect of his counsel would bring. It is not, except in style, a courtly production. Darnley probably could not, but Mary certainly both could and would see the poet's drift, and happy would it have been for both had they avoided the faults against which the poet directed his pointed admonition.

If James turned out 'the wisest fool in Christendom,' the folly was not the fault of Buchanan, but of James's nature, and perhaps also of flatterers of the 'Mester Peter Young' order, who scattered tares among the wheat of the more worthy sower. At all events he made James a scholar, if the latter made himself a pedant; and this implied, in the circumstances and the particular case, an exercise of firm and even stern discipline—of which a famous if not quite elegant instance has been quoted above,—and which was better fitted to improve the *morale* of the pupil than the fortunes of the disciplinarian. As Melville puts it, Buchanan 'held the king in awe,' an awe which James felt and resented to the last, although, to do him justice, he also plumed himself on his training by an unrivalled scholar. Three works remarkable for their political teaching—his *Baptistes*, his *De Jure Regni*, and his *History*—Buchanan dedicated to James, in prefaces as remarkable as the works themselves. All three books were mainly, the second entirely, motived by the idea which Buchanan seems to have regarded as constituting and directing his true mission in life, namely, the unspeakable value of liberty, the constant possibility and deadly evil of tyranny, and the corresponding and always pressing duty of forestalling this possibility and resisting this evil by abundant proclamation and practice of the doctrine that legitimate political sovereignty exists only for the good and by the will of the people—a principle, of course, entirely subversive of the despotic doctrine of the Divine right of kings, so prevalent in usurpationist quarters in that day, and anticipatory of the modern and accepted democratic 'platform' of 'Government of the People, by the People, for the People.'

This is not the stage at which to describe the books themselves—it is their prefaces that make them relevant at present,—but a word to indicate their general character is necessary. The *Baptistes* was written (1540-41) when Buchanan was comparatively a young man, thirty-four or thirty-five, and was 'regenting' in a great secondary school or gymnasium at Bordeaux, called the Collège de Guyenne, organised and presided over by one André de Gouvéa, a famous Portuguese Humanist and educator of the day. This *Baptistes* was simply a dramatic reproduction of the story of John the Baptist and his tragic end, the *dramatis personæ* being King Herod, Queen Herodias, the latter's dancing daughter, Malchus the high priest, Gamaliel, and the unlucky John himself. It was composed, Buchanan tells us in the dedicatory preface and in his autobiography (1574), in accordance with the rules of the college, and intended by him to win the students, who acted it, from the silly 'mysteries' of the monks to the imitation of classic antiquity, and the rising study of religion in its original documents. But there was something more intended. It is scarcely necessary to read 'between the lines' to find a complete condemnation of absolutist tyranny, and a picture of the misery which it brings on the tyrant himself as well as on his victims. This was not the kind of writing to please monarchs of the period. Nevertheless Buchanan dedicates it (1576) to the boy-king, as 'having a peculiar appositeness to his position,' warning him of 'the agonisings and wretchedness which await tyrants, even when they seem to be most flourishing outwardly.'

This lesson, he goes on to say, he thinks 'not only useful, but absolutely essential,' for his royal pupil to learn now, so that he may 'early begin to hate' a fault which 'he ought always to shun.' Moreover, he 'wishes to place it on record, for the information of posterity, that if the king should in the future, at the instigation of evil advisers, or by allowing the lust of power to overcome the principles of his education, act contrary to the warnings now given him, the blame must be laid, not on his teachers, but on himself, in not having listened to those who gave him good counsel.' This was not the language of flattery; and though James was only ten when he was thus addressed, the precocity of his intelligence would enable him to understand its import. He was destined, in a very few years, to be king in fact as he was now in name, and Buchanan knew that if his charge turned out other than he was trying to make him—what actually happened—his own plain speaking would not be to his advantage. Knowing this, he did his duty, and had his sovereign for his enemy when the latter got used to being his own master. The fact reveals an elevation of character in Buchanan which cannot be justly forgotten in judging of him in other connections. It is not surprising that the agents in Scotland of Cecil, Queen Elizabeth's great minister, when on the look-out for 'Biencontents,' as they were called, who might be dealt with in the way of bribery with a view to forming a strong Elizabethan party in Scotland, should have secretly reported (1579, King's age thirteen) Buchanan as 'a singular man,' while of 'Mester Peter Young' they say that he was 'specially well affected, and ready to persuade the king to be in favour of her majestye.'

Three years after dedicating the *Baptistes* to James in the style we have seen, he dedicated the *De Jure* to him (1579). This was a still bolder and more independent proceeding. Without entering, for the present, into the details of its argument, it may be enough to remember that, with its doctrine of

Sovereignty as originating from the People, existing for their benefit, and not autocratic, but bounded by laws to which the People have consented, the *De Jure* must have appeared to Absolutist and 'Divine right people' generally, revolutionary rubbish of the most pernicious description; and accordingly, in 1584, when Buchanan had been dead two years, they had it condemned and its publication and circulation forbidden by express Statute of the Scots Parliament—the King, of course, assenting, if not inciting; while, as we have already seen, the University of Oxford, later on, paid it the compliment of having it publicly burned. Buchanan must have, in a general way, foreseen the possibility of something like this, and the risk he ran if the King should, in his riper age, turn upon him and seek to rend him. This, however, did not deter him from pressing his democratic treatise on the attention and study of his royal pupil.

He praises him, not in the fulsome and fawning language of the Dedication literature of the time, but with evident sincerity and honest, hearty admiration for the brightness of his abilities, his intellectual interests, his independence of judgment while inquiring into the truth of things and opinions. He congratulates him, too, on his present aversion to flattery, that 'nurse of Tyranny, and deadliest of plagues to genuine kingship'—*tyrannidis nutricula, et legitimi regni gravissima pestis,*—and rejoices that he seems 'instinctively to detest'—*naturæ quodam instinctu oderis*—'the courtly solecisms and barbarisms'—*solæcismos et barbarismos aulicos*—affected by those self-chosen 'arbiters of elegance'—*elegantiæ censores*—who 'spice their conversation'—*velut sermonis condimenta*—with 'profuse employment of "Your Majesty," "Your Lordship," "Your Illustrious Highness," and any other still more sickening title they can find'—*passim* Majestates, Dominationes, Illustritates, *et si qua alia magis sunt putida, adspergant.* Was there any latent reference here to 'Mester Peter Young' and his courtier ways? Anyhow, Buchanan plainly owns that he has doubts and fears for James's future. He tells him of the dangers of evil companionship, and invites him to the study of the essay thus dedicated to him, not only as an instructor that will show him the right and wrong of the subject, but as a Mentor that may 'keep at him' in importunate and even audacious fashion, as it may seem for the moment. If he is faithful to the principles commended to him, there will be peace in the present for him and his, and lasting glory in the future. James subsequently thought he could do better, and threw off his early training; but, notwithstanding, or in consequence, he failed alike to achieve a peaceful career or to transmit a glorious memory. The citation from the chorus in the *Thyestes* of Seneca—who also was tutor to a royal failure, although James must, of course, be admitted to have been a brilliant success compared with Nero—in which the great but ill-starred

Roman delineates the Stoic king, appended to Buchanan's dedication, no doubt expresses his own view of what James might and should have been: beginning with—

> 'Regem non faciunt opes
> Non vestis Tyriæ color,' etc.

> 'It is not wealth nor the purple robe that makes a king,' etc.

and ending—

> 'Rex est, qui metuit nihil,
> Rex est, qui cupiet nihil.
> Hoc regnum sibi quisque dat.'

> 'He is a king who has conquered Fear and Desire. Such a kingship every man may give himself, and none else.'

It is in the same spirit that he dedicates his *History* to the King (1582, James sixteen). He knows perfectly well how his book is likely to be taken. Writing (1577) to Sir Thomas Randolph, Queen Elizabeth's representative at the Scottish court, and Buchanan's *quondam* pupil at Paris, he says: 'I am occupiit in wryting of our historie, being assurit to content few, and to displease many thairthrow.' Among the many 'displeased,' he could not but foresee that possibly the young King might be found, on account of the unfavourable view which, in common with most historians, he felt himself obliged to take of the character and career of the King's own mother, Queen Mary. He must have felt too that, unless James were all the more magnanimous, he might take deep offence—as he did, death alone saving Buchanan from criminal proceedings on account of his 'seditious' writings—at his now nominal preceptor's contention that by the Constitution of Scotland the monarchy had, as an historical fact as well as by a true philosophy, been all along a derivative and limited, even very limited, one, and anything but a divinely authorised Absolutism, as maintained by courtly authorities. Buchanan, however, prefers to assume that James had enough of the king and the public man in him to sink private feeling in public duty and accept truth, however unpleasant; and accordingly he dedicates his *History* to him, urging him to follow the example of his good predecessors and eschew that of the bad ones, and more particularly commending to his notice and imitation the career of the saintly David I., the 'sair saunt for the crown' of one of his successors and descendants, as a ruler who, according to his lights—some of which, however, especially those that led to his profuse and corrupting liberality to the Church, Buchanan, herein endorsing John Major, his early

St. Andrews 'regent' in Logic, emphatically decries—devoted himself not to pleasure, or the strengthening of his prerogative, but to what seemed to him to be the true welfare of his people. In all this, some of Buchanan's critics have thought him too stern, and that gentler methods might have won over James to better thoughts. But truth must always be stern to those who dislike or fear it. Yet those only are the real friends of these latter who give them the chance of profiting by it; and in so acting by James, come what might of himself and his personal fortunes, Buchanan will be thought by most admirers of a high *morale* to have stamped himself as a wholly high-minded and even heroic character.

CHAPTER IV
FURTHER CHARACTERISTICS

A Stoic Philosopher

We are now, perhaps, in a better position to face Melville's further characterisation of him as a 'Stoik philosopher, of gud religion for a poet.' That Sir James knew something about Stoicism, although perhaps not very deeply, is shown by his apparent familiarity with the Seneca, whom he quotes in that remarkable preface of his, although only for a sarcastic comment upon those foolish political Stoics who, like Sir James himself, throw away their Stoical honesty upon unappreciative 'Princes,' and repent of their Stoicism when too late. That Buchanan had studied the Stoics goes without saying. He was as familiar with the metres of Seneca and Boëtius as with those of Horace and Catullus, and he was not the man—not the pedant or grammarian—to master the form and style merely of his author without penetrating to his inner thought. How minutely he had read Cicero appears from his famous emendation in the second Philippic of *patrem tuum*, passed over by previous commentators, into *matrem*, subsequently *parentem tuam*—a case in which even Gibbon would probably have admitted that a vowel, to say nothing of a diphthong, was vital to truth, and which gave occasion to Dionysius Lambinus to flay alive a rival Ciceronic editor, Petrus Victorius by name, for critical larceny, in having feloniously but silently appropriated, first, the laurels of Buchanan who did the good deed, and next, those of him, Lambinus, who had the sagacity to recognise and adopt Buchanan's great performance. But Buchanan had doubtless read Cicero's *De Officiis* with not less care, and had gathered from its pages some idea of Stoicism as expounded by Cicero's own early tutor, Panætius, probably the most distinguished of Rome's then professional teachers of this great ethical system. He must have come across such a passage as this, where Cicero says: 'What is called the *summum bonum* by the Stoics, to live agreeably to Nature (*convenienter Naturæ vivere*), has, I conceive, this meaning—always to conform to virtue; and as to all other things which may be according to Nature (*secundum naturam*) [*i.e.* other possible *bona* besides the *summum*: as gratifications of appetite, propensity, ambition, etc.], to take them if they should not be repugnant to virtue,'—a declaration which Butler, with his supremacy of conscience as part of true Nature, would have accepted, and in substance, indeed, has explicitly endorsed. Probably, too, he had noticed the habitual doctrine of Epictetus, 'this is the great task of life also, to discern things and divide them, and say, "Outward things are not in my power; to will is in my power. Where shall I seek the Good, and where the Evil? Within me—in all that is my own. But of all that is alien to thee, call nothing good nor evil, nor profitable nor hurtful, nor any such term as these. What then? should we be careless of such things? In no wise. For this, again, is a vice in the Will, and thus contrary to Nature. But be at once careful, because the use of things is not indifferent, and steadfast and tranquil because the things themselves are.... And hard it is, indeed, to mingle and reconcile together the carefulness of one whom outward things affect, with the steadfastness of him who regards them not. But impossible it is not; and if it is, it is impossible to be happy.... Take example of dice-players. The numbers are indifferent, the dice are indifferent. How can I tell what may be thrown up? But carefully and skilfully to make use of what is thrown, that is where my proper business begins"' (Rolleston translation).

This seems to me to describe the general temper and spirit in which Buchanan confronted the vicissitudes of life. I do not say that in a Register of Religions like that provided under 6 and 7 Will. IV. c. 85 and amending acts, he would have entered himself as 'G. B., Stoic.' For one thing, he had not the chance, as only one denomination was allowed. Nor do I think he ever said in his heart, 'I am a Stoic, and mean to guide my life by the Stoical system'; but all the same, I believe that *convenienter naturæ vivere*, interpreted in the Stoical sense, sank with gradually increasing depth into his moral nature as life went on, and preserved him from Epicurean timidity, levity, and egotism. Not that he succeeded perfectly, but he kept trying to. Stoicism did not, any more than Christianity, maintain that the concrete Stoic was free from sins, both of omission and commission. Not Socrates, nor even Diogenes—most misunderstood of men, who attained the high degree of Cynic—would have been claimed as impeccable, although they came very near it. It has been said that Buchanan in several ways allowed the 'outward things that were not in his power' get the better of the 'will' that was, that he was, for instance, fiery and irritable, for little other reason, apparently, than that he had Celtic blood in him, and was bound to be so; that he was disappointed and soured by his early struggle with poverty, his critics assuming that this must have been the case, because in his circumstances they would have been so themselves; that he was a 'good hater'—as if that were really a fault at all, etc.

Had he been all that his detractors call him, that would not have unstoicised him, since, as already said, the system admits that 'no mere man is able to keep the commandments, but doth daily break them,' as the Shorter Catechism puts it in questionable grammar. But his censors have not sufficiently observed that if he displayed faults of passion, eagerness, temper, impatience, it was when he was young; and the fair inference is that if he overcame those tendencies as life proceeded, it was by a persistent effort of 'will,' repelling the invading influence of the 'outward.' By all accounts his age was not a 'crabbed age.' Though plain, and even rustic, in appearance—in the matter of dress he seems to have carried his superiority to the 'outward' to a really unstoical extreme—when he opened his mouth he was a different being, courtly in manner, refined and elegant in expression, humorous and entertaining, as well as instructive even to the verge of 'edifying,' in every way a polite and variously pleasant companion— 'with nothing of the pedagogue about him but the gown,' said a keen and competent observer, who knew him well. 'Plaisant in company,' says the slightly garrulous Sir James, 'rehersing at all occasions moralities short and fecfull, whereof he had aboundance, and invented wher he wanted'—a combination, in short, of wit, wisdom, resource, and pith, anything but a picture of the snappish old curmudgeon, soured and made ill-natured by disappointments which he had not wisely overcome. His letters, too, of which unfortunately we possess only a few, reveal the same well-ordered and placid moral interior: full of the purest friendly devotion, ready always to do a good turn, especially to merit in obscurity, not insensible to the difficulties and distresses of life, but rising above them, and achieving in spite of them not only contentment, but a degree of light-heartedness. He was long a martyr to gout—a sore affliction, if sufferers from it may be trusted. But he took it with a smile. Writing (1577) at seventy-one to his old friend and pupil Randolph, by that time Postmaster-General to Queen Elizabeth, he tells him that he is hard at work on his *History*, and adds: 'The rest of my occupation is wyth the gout, quhilk holdis me besy both day and nyt. And quhair ye say ye haif not lang to lyif [live], I traist [trust] to God to go before you, albeit I be on fut, and ye ryd the *post*.... And thus I tak my leif [leave] shortly at you now, and my lang leif quhen God pleasis.' The fun may not be of a side-splitting character, nor the seriousness very unctuous, but the man who could encounter the gout keeping at him night and day in this fashion, must have practised keeping the 'outward' at bay in a considerable variety of situations, and for a considerable time, and with considerable success.

The fastidious Sir James seems to think that Buchanan rather stepped down from the high 'Stoik philosopher' pedestal in being what he calls 'extrem vengeable against any man that had offendit him.' But, as already suggested, Dr. Johnson, who was a tolerable authority on the higher morality, would have been rather prejudiced in Buchanan's favour on this very account, and would probably have wished to know Sir James's evidence for unfavourably meant reflection, and would certainly have thought that it did not amount to much. It may be pardoned in an old ex-courtier to think it a dreadful thing to have written 'dispytfull invectives against the Erle of Monteith.' No doubt, the fact that the subject of the incriminated 'invectives' was some 'particulaires that was between him (the "Erle") and the Laird of Buchwhennen,' would dispose Buchanan to do his best, because blood is thicker than water, and when Buchanan was at his best on an invective, it is likely enough that the object of it and his friends might think it 'dispytfull,' if not worse, although unprejudiced people might find it very good reading. But everything depends on the merits of the 'particulaires,' and of these Sir James tells us nothing. With every respect to him and his kidney, an 'Erle' may be in the wrong while a 'Laird' is in the right, and if that were so in the present instance, it was the part of a 'philosopher,' and especially a 'Stoik' one, to take an 'Erle' precisely for what he was worth and no more, as Diogenes, the champion Stoic, in the famous anecdote, whether *vero* or *ben trovato*, tells Alexander the Great that, as far as he knew, the only thing he (the Great) could do for him (the champion) was to stand out of his light.

Sir James's other instance of Buchanan's 'vengeableness' is not much more to the point. Perhaps the story of the requisitioned 'hackney' that was 'sa sur of foot and sa easy' is not true, and merely an instance of the baseless gossip that so easily gets into circulation about distinguished people, and people that are not distinguished as well. But even if the 'said horse' and Melville's history of it are facts, most people will be of opinion that Buchanan had grounds of displeasure. He was deprived of the 'said horse'—there is no word of a price, but that is immaterial—for public purposes during the civil wars. When the public purpose was satisfied, the animal ought to have been returned to him. In the meantime Morton had 'bocht' the beast, apparently from the requisitioner or his donee, and Morton was not the man to pay too much for him. But when the morally rightful proprietor applied to have his own back, and that time after time, he found the Regent of Scotland standing upon his real or fancied contractual rights. If Buchanan and Morton were the great friends Melville says they were, Buchanan was not treated in a friendly manner. It takes two to make a friendship, and by the proverb it is 'giff gaff,' not giff and no gaff, that creates the connection. 'Love me, love my dog,' is one thing; but love me, and let me love your horse *à la Morton*, is very much another thing. Loyalty is tested by conduct in small matters, even more than in great ones, and in the circumstances stated, it would not have been wonderful if Buchanan's feeling of personal liking for Morton, if it ever existed, underwent a change. It is certain that Buchanan at a particular point ceased to approve of parts of Morton's policy, but not for any such trumpery reason as the one assigned by tattling Sir James. While Knox was alive, there was a complete solidarity of public action between him and Morton and Buchanan, to whom the cause of Protestantism meant the cause of liberty. Their aim was to strengthen the position of Protestantism in Scotland by the English Alliance, and to strengthen the position of Elizabeth as fighting the general battle of Protestantism against the Catholic reaction of the Continent; while, even in spite of Elizabeth herself, who had an interest in Monarchical Absolutism as well as in Protestant freedom, they firmly resisted every attempt to restore Mary, the champion of the old faith and its political tyranny.

With this view Knox, who was a statesman, and not the mere crazy fanatic and demagogue that he is sometimes mistaken for, winked at the moral irregularities of Morton, and would even have joined the General Assembly in making him an 'Elder,' if he had not himself, though quite free from scruples, felt that this would have been putting on rather too much; while Buchanan gave him every support in his power, and as internal evidence shows, wrote for him the Memorial demanded by Elizabeth at the final London Conference, in which the right of the Scottish nation to depose Mary from her regal office is defended on the same principles and often in the same language as are employed in the *Detectio*, the *De Jure*, the *History*, and indeed all through Buchanan's writings. After Knox's death he still pursued the anti-Marian and pro-Elizabethan policy, but with a difference. To complete the unity of Scottish and English Protestantism, Morton sought to reduce the Scottish Church to the same level with the English—that is, to make it Episcopal and Erastian. When he made this proposal he was fully aware of the opposition on which he had to reckon; for although he made very light of the other Presbyterian clergy, and indeed told some of them who kept boring him beyond endurance that he might have some of them 'hanged' if they did not take care, he knew that in Knox he met a man who was not afraid of him, or any one, or anything else, and who was the one man in Scotland who was a stronger man than himself.

But when Knox was gone, he had the stage to himself, and began to develop his views, apparently seeking to use Buchanan as a tool for carrying them into execution. James Melville, in his entertaining diary, tells us that when Andrew his uncle returned from abroad, Morton sent Buchanan to him to try whether the influence of an old master over an old pupil and lifelong friend could not prevail on Andrew to assist him in more or less Anglicising the 'Kirk.' The idea of getting Andrew Melville to assent to Episcopacy and Erastianism, or any modification of them, was of course utterly futile and ludicrous. You might as well have tried to marry fire and water. To Buchanan himself the proposal would not appear unreasonable in itself. He was not an ecclesiastic, but a scholar and thinker to whom the struggle between Presbyterian and Prelate would appear a sectarian squabble, but his interview with his severely Puritanical pupil undoubtedly convinced him that Morton's scheme for turning the Scottish into a branch of the Anglican church would simply defeat itself. It would rend and desolate the ecclesiastical life of Scotland—as was too amply proved by the Scottish history of the seventeenth century,—and paralyse it for the time as a power in resisting the efforts of the avowed or tacit Catholic League to crush that element of liberty in the Protestant revolt, which to Buchanan was its most valuable characteristic. This, and not 'the said horse,' was unquestionably the explanation of Buchanan's growing antagonism to Morton. If 'the said horse' was not a myth, it might, taken in conjunction with the abortive Melville negotiation, lead Buchanan to think that Morton was just a little too much disposed to convert his friends into useful instruments for his own purposes—an impression which would be greatly deepened when he noticed Morton's great and increasing anxiety to get the young King, Buchanan's special charge, into his power, Buchanan's opposition to which project, for which Melville (Sir James) expressly vouches, contributed ultimately to Morton's downfall.

But that Buchanan, from the alleged 'hackney' period, and from 'hackney' causes, 'spak evil' of Morton 'in all places and at all occasions,' is not only incredible when we remember the high character and intellectual tastes of the man, but inconsistent with the facts of the situation. If Buchanan had desired to abuse Morton in a vindictive spirit, he had the amplest opportunity in his *History*. But what are the facts? There is not a word of depreciation, but many of praise, more or less direct. He does full justice to Morton's great powers and wise foresight, and in accordance with a rule which he held ought to be applied to public men, screens his defects. He describes him exactly as he was, a fearless and skilful military leader, and a sagacious, firm, and patriotic statesman. He even goes out of his way a little to state facts in Morton's favour, recording the energy and self-sacrifice which he once and again displayed in rising from a sick-bed of very serious prostration and redeeming a dangerous crisis to which he knew no one else was equal, and in relating the last negotiations which Morton conducted with Elizabeth and her council pays a due compliment to his diplomatic dexterity and merit. Detractors have said that he stopped in his *History* when on the threshold of Morton's Regency, because he did not wish to advertise an adversary. But it was really death, not animosity, that stayed the narrator's hand. By a weird prescience, Buchanan forecast the hour of his exit from time to a nicety, if such a term may be employed in such a connection. He worked up to within a month of his death; and then, when asked whether he meant to go on with his work, he said he had now another work to do; and when further asked what that was, he said it was the work of 'dying,' to which he addressed himself in the fashion we have already seen — a fashion not unworthy of a 'Stoik philosopher.'

Not so Facile

It is of course a pity that we do not possess an account and criticism of Morton's singularly able and interesting rule in Scotland by so original a contemporary observer as Buchanan. That it would, in all respects, have been favourable, is not likely, for the reasons already noticed. That it would have been consciously unjust is incredible in the light of such treatment of Morton by Buchanan as we have, much of which must have been written after Morton's violent and unjust execution. Indeed, one could almost wish to be sure that the 'hackney' story was true, as it would show how superior the 'Stoik philosopher' can rise to petty and personal considerations when he has to discharge the high function of narrator and judge of public events. That his delineation of men and events would have been conspicuously able is as certain as any such matter can be, notwithstanding good Sir James's remark that 'in his auld dayes he was become sleperie and cairless, and followed in many things the vulgair oppinion, for he was naturally populaire,' etc. There is no sign of this alleged falling off into sleepiness and carelessness in Buchanan's *History*. The last chapter is as well thought out and written as the first. You may think him wrong, but you can have no doubt about the distinctness of his explanation of the sequence of events and the motives and aims of historic characters, while the style in no respect falls below the unsurpassed standard of prose Latinity maintained throughout the entire work. One grows a little suspicious of Sir James's judgment when his reasons for it are considered. Buchanan had come, he says, to 'follow in many things the vulgair oppinion, *for* he was naturally populaire'; that is to say, he was democratic in spirit. Of course he was. He felt it to be his mission in life to oppose Regal Absolutism in behalf of public liberty, and never let slip an opportunity of maintaining that all sovereignty originated from the people, and was justifiable only as it subserved their advantage. The courtly Sir James did not like this. He was a good deal of what Thackeray has immortalised as a 'Snob.' He might very well be called Sir 'Jeames,' and when he says Buchanan had been 'maid factious,' we must not forget that the 'faction' Sir J. had in his eye was the 'faction' of Liberty against Tyranny, and how far that can be justly called a faction will be settled by different critics according to their different tastes.

With his soreness on this point, it is not surprising that he should describe Buchanan as 'easily abused, and sa facill that he was led with any company that he hanted for the tyme,' and that 'he spak and wret as they that were about him for the tym informed him.' That is to say, Buchanan did not belong to Sir J.'s 'set,' which is not surprising. The Democratic old scholar and thinker was not likely to sympathise with the kind of people whom the courtier naturally regarded as the *élite* of society and the salt of the earth. Knox and Scaliger, Moray and Mar, Randolph and Ascham, Melville and Scrymgeour, Beza and Tycho Brahé, were among his correspondents or intimates; and if Buchanan thought that 'information' derived from persons of that stamp was *prima facie* trustworthy, it was no more than the rules of evidence permitted and justified. It is barely conceivable that they sought to 'abuse' him and succeeded, but specific proof of this is necessary in such a case, and is not forthcoming. That Buchanan was 'sa facill that he was led with any company that he hanted for the tyme' is rendered utterly incredible by the facts. It is one of the most remarkable circumstances in Buchanan's career that he mixed with people of the most opposite and irreconcilable characters and positions, while preserving his independence of both. There was, for instance, a time when he was equally at home with Maitland and Moray, and what is more wonderful still, with Knox and Mary. On the very same day when he had been reading Livy and turning verses with Mary at Holyrood, he might be discussing Calvin and the political situation with Knox in his High Street house; and what is more, each of them knew it. To my mind this does not point to 'facility,' but to dominancy. The 'Stoik philosopher' was quietly their master, because he was his own. He was not moved by their inter-personal attractions and repulsions, but passionlessly contemplated them as interesting life-'forces,' that he had to take as they came along, and in his calm judicial presence they bowed their more vehement heads. That is as probable an explanation as any of a very striking psychological phenomenon.

'Gud Religion'

'He was also of gud religion for a poet,' says Sir James, when adding the last item to the creditor side of his profit and loss account of Buchanan's qualities. 'Gud religion for a poet' is good, and characteristic of the times which said *Ubi tres medici, duo athei,*—'Three Physicists,[4] two Atheists.' Humanists, and still more Humanist poets, were also suspect, and for the same reason. The rebellion against Scholasticism, the resuscitation of the old Pagan spirit in thought and art and science, involved a staggering blow to Ecclesiastical Faith. Men whose minds were steeped in the literature of ancient Greece and Rome could not take sympathetically, I will not say, to Christianity, but to the dogmatic system of the Church, and even to much of its ethical teaching. 'Humanity,' in the sense of 'the humanities,' really meant the antithesis of Divinity. The Renaissance was a wakening up of the human intellect, an assertion of 'private judgment' in every possible sphere of its exercise, and in innumerable instances the Humanist created a faith and a code of morals for himself, although for comfort and convenience he might conceal his spiritual interior from the view of the ignorant and the unenlightened. In many an instance he held that there was one law for the men who understand, and another for the 'vulgar' who cannot understand. Popes and priests were often at heart Humanists of the most 'advanced' type, pushing the right of 'private judgment' to its furthest limit, discarding the public creed, and in morals, exercising, in favour of their appetites, that dispensing power which 'private judgment,' the Pope's successor in so many awakened intellects, carried over with it, at all events extensively into practice, while simultaneously a silent outward conformity with the established system was carefully maintained.

Not that it did not sometimes betray itself. It is a Roman dignitary who is credited with the famous remark about the profit brought in by 'this fable of Christ'; and everybody remembers how horrified poor Luther was in Rome when he heard the priests at Mass saying *panis es, panis manebis,—* 'bread thou art, and bread thou shalt remain.' The open licentiousness of many Church dignitaries of those days is too notorious for special mention. 'Private judgment' may be a primary human right and a duty owing by reason to itself of the highest order; but to cast off in its favour an inveterate obedience to authority, is a psychological problem surrounded with the greatest difficulty and danger, and unless when under the control of an adequately strong judgment and will, may cause much wreckage of faith and conduct. I do not think that Buchanan suffered much in this way—certainly not so much as many others among the leaders and supporters of the Reformation; while any damage he sustained was amply compensated by his gains. Knox and other Reformers—I speak of Scotland—were driven by the violence of the recoil involved in their assault on the Catholic and Feudal system into extreme positions, necessarily harmful to themselves, and bequeathing legacies of disadvantage to their successors.

They needed, through polemical necessities, an authority equal to that of Rome, which they had overthrown, and this drove them into placing Scripture in a position which the speculative and historical criticism of the last two centuries has made highly uncomfortable for many people of intelligence, including Broad Churchmen, whom it has driven into crypto-scepticism, and Evangelicals and Ritualists, whom it has moulded into wilful believers. Their denunciation and destruction of 'idolatry' and every rite 'not appointed in the Word,' with the necessity they lay under of maintaining a high standard of Biblical morality as a proof that Antinomian licence was not the necessary result of Justification by Faith, engaged them in a war against Art, Literature, and Natural Beauty and Pleasure, which, while it stamped the national consciousness with a grave, deep, and serious habit of regarding life, which is of the greatest value, produced also an immense amount, not yet exorcised, of official Pharisaism, popular hypocrisy, and practical pessimism, with all its miserable consequences. These were unfortunate results of the great rebellion against authority and claim of 'private judgment,' apparently suggested, in part at least, by self-defence; while the Nicene and Predestinarian dogmas were put forward with an emphasis and detail which would not be attempted in the present day, but were very seasonable in times when immaculate and even strained orthodoxy was both weapon and armour in a degree that does not prevail now.

Knox, it must be remembered, did not discourage the belief that he could predict the future and had a good deal of the 'second-sight' in him. He had a powerful political instinct, and he and his chief associates knew that if they went 'too far' in their destructions, the alarm would be taken, and the life and death struggle in which they were engaged would for them be lost for ever; and every man of any depth of thought or feeling is aware that the 'doctrines of grace,' in their inner, perhaps mystical, interpretation, and apart altogether from the stupendous metaphysical and historical setting assigned them in systems of Christian dogma, have a consoling, strengthening, and guiding influence on that vast body of serious, simple, if often practically powerful natures, to whom Criticism is neither a necessity nor a possibility. Such a union of accommodation and exaggeration need not be construed as of set purpose propositional in form, and deliberate in execution. In the transition from authority to private judgment initiated by Humanism and the Renaissance generally, special Reformation exigencies may be conceived as leading to such a union, so that in thought and action it was only semi-conscious and instinctive, and there was little time for the minutiæ of introspective scrutiny. On the ethical side, however, there was no Renaissance loosening among the mass of the leading Reformers. The value of the controversial mendacities propagated about the morals of Knox may be judged of by the fact that the coryphæus of the revilers maintained that he won his second wife by magic! As a rule they kept the ten commandments, and especially the seventh, rigidly. They failed a good deal on the new one of Charity. They preached the 'Gospel' with technical accuracy, but they mostly practised the 'Law,' and if Paul had returned among them, he would probably have re-edited his Epistle to the Romans, with up-to-date applications, as indeed he might have to do still.

CHAPTER V
BUCHANAN AND CALVINISM

In Buchanan's case, the revolt from authority seems to have produced different effects. As regards dogma, it appears to have led him into an attitude of mind that was mainly negative. He had none of the 'Evangelical' fervour which marked the utterances of Knox, Luther, Calvin though to a less degree, and the Reforming preachers of Scotland. He never preached, in the popular sense of the word, although as Principal of St. Leonard's and 'doctor in the schools' he could easily have had himself 'called' and ordained, if he had been animated by any zeal for the function. He could not have written such letters as Knox wrote, full of pious sentiment and sympathy, in phraseology that was absolutely unctuous, to Mrs. Bowes, and Mrs. Locke, and other women, who leant on him for a sort of semi-priestly or confessorial guidance. He was a critic, not a sentimentalist. You may read his whole works through, prose and poetry both, without knowing that he laid any stress on the Calvinism of the Scottish Church, except on its destructive side. Indeed, much of his literary work was done before he openly and formally broke with Rome, which he was in no hurry to do. He satirises the clergy, especially the monks, and ridicules such doctrines as those of Indulgences and Transubstantiation, the latter especially in the *Franciscanus*, where it is stated with a grossness and extravagance of literalism which would probably be disowned by the highest order of Catholic dogmatist. As the *Franciscanus* was published, after revision and completion, in his Protestant days, this may have been an addition of the period; but nowhere, in anything he wrote during the Protestant part of his career, does he emphasise, or almost even allude to, such doctrines as Justification by Faith, the Incarnation, the Atonement, Election, and Reprobation, or any of the positive dogmatic propositions most prominently characteristic of Scottish Protestantism.

Not a Zealot

It is remarkable that in his *History* he associates the Reformers less with *Evangelium* than with *Libertas*. They are the *vindices libertatis* — 'the champions of liberty' — quite as much or oftener than the *Evangelii professores* — 'the professors of the Evangel,'—from which it might seem that for Buchanan, not the least valuable aspect of Protestantism lay in its being a struggle for liberty—a view in which a good many other people will be ready to concur. Queen Mary, in her later years, protesting against Buchanan's appointment as her son's tutor, described him, in writing, as an 'Atheist'; but that was in the sense in which Athanasius described Arius as an atheist, and is said to have seized an opportunity of striking him in the jaw in that capacity, to show what he thought of it and him. Arius, however, constantly professed himself a believer in 'God, the Father Almighty,' under, of course, 'heretical' modifications; but Athanasius thought that a wrong God—that is, a God that was not God, according to Athanasius—was no God, and spoke and acted accordingly. Buchanan was certainly no atheist in his own sense and intention, which, it must always be remembered, was essentially of a deep-sea seriousness, although the wavelets of wit might often dance and gleam on its surface. He manifestly held by some Almighty Power called by him God, *Deus, Numen, Providentia*; but whether this was the God of Mary Stuart, or the anthropomorphic God of Calvin, or the accommodation to the popular sense of reverence ascribed by many people, and not without reason, to Carlyle, might form a subject of discussion.

Bearing on this matter, passing allusion may be made to the Dirge or *Epicedium*, as he called it, which Buchanan wrote on the death of Calvin (1564), an event which occurred some three years, more or less, after Buchanan had publicly become a Protestant, when he was already a member of the General Assembly, sitting cheek-by-jowl with Knox, and on the Assembly's judicial committee; the year when Mary, having been finally off with the Spanish Don Carlos marriage, was drawing towards the Catholic Darnley marriage, which Knox, correctly scenting on the way, was beginning to anathematise by anticipation, he having the year before fiercely denounced from the High Kirk pulpit the Spanish alliance as fatal to Scotland, because it was an 'infidel' marriage, and 'all Papists are infidels,' said the uncompromising one, in the true Athanasian vein, on the head of which he had quarrelled with Mary and Moray also; while all the time Buchanan was, to Knox's knowledge, continuing to act as Mary's Court poet, and possibly meditating on the 'Pompa' or masque for her wedding, and getting on so well with her that she was arranging for giving him that £500 (Scots) pension from Crossraguel Abbey, out of which it cost him such excruciating difficulty to get anything at all, at the same time that he was helping the General Assembly to revise the *Book of Discipline*, translating Spanish despatches for the Privy Council, and generally acting as 'handy man' on the highest planes all round. This 'Dirge' is too long for quotation: a curious attempt to combine the Pagan spirit and the Calvinistic theology—

spiritual elevation and sarcastic wit in the best poetic form. 'Those who believe that there are no *Manes*, *i.e.* no hereafter, or if they do, live despising Pluto and the trans-Stygian penalties, may well deplore their coming fate, while they leave sorrow to surviving friends. But we have no such grief over our lost Calvin. He has passed beyond the stars, and, filled with a draught of Deity (*Numinis*), lives in an eternal and nearer enjoyment of "God" (*Deo*). But Death has not taken all of him from us. We have monuments of his genius and his fame wherever the Reformed religion has spread. We have the terror which he struck, and which his name will continue to strike, into your Popes—your Clements and Pauls, and Juliuses and Piuses; while we know that the Pontiff tyrant of fire and sword who appropriated all the functions of the nether kingdom—becoming a Pluto in empire, a Harpy in his shameful extortions, a Fury in his martyr-making fire, a Charon in his viaticum (*Charon naulo*), and a Cerberus in his mitre (*triplici corona Cerberus*)—will have to appropriate the penalties also of the same lower world, becoming a Tantalus thirsty amidst waters, a Sisyphus rolling back the ever-recurring stone, a Prometheus with vultures ceaselessly pecking at his liver, a Danaid vainly filling her empty bucket, and an Ixion twisted into a circle on his endless wheel.'

À propos of Calvin's 'draught of Deity,' Buchanan gives in the course of the poem what seems to be meant for an explanation of the spiritual work of 'regeneration,' which, I am afraid, would not have been so satisfactory to Mess John Davidson as some others of his efforts to propitiate that sound divine. As the soul animates the body, otherwise a mass of clay—*sic animi Deus est animus*—so '"God" is the Soul of the soul,' and when the *Numinis haustus*, the 'draught of Deity,' has been taken, the soul which before was 'shrouded in darkness, illusioned by empty appearance, and grasping at mere shadows of the "right and good,"' sees the 'darkness disappear, the vain "simulacra" cease, the unveiled face of "truth" reveal itself in light.' I may be wrong, but this looks to me more like a Pantheistic theory of 'illumination' than the 'regeneration' of the Calvinistic creeds! Besides, there is no word of 'sin,' and the change to at least an incipient 'holiness' only from '*illusion*' to 'truth' (*verum*). If it be said that this must be assumed, then a new contradiction of Calvinism arises, since a divine Soul of the soul cannot will evil, and 'sanctification' is thus erroneously made out to be an instantaneous act and not a gradual process. Altogether, and as it stands, the passage might have been written by one of those later Stoics, including possibly Aurelius himself, who seem to have believed in the indwelling Divinity, and that the souls of good men at death were not immediately reabsorbed into the All, but lived with 'God,' in some cases a thousand years, in others for ever, or, at all events, until the 'philosopher's year' was over, and the new cycle began to repeat the history of the old.

But there is one omission which, among various others, seems remarkable. Of the relics enumerated by Buchanan as left by Calvin, he passes over the most important of all—Calvin's own body. He makes no reference to the resurrection. Yet, on orthodox principles, Calvin's glory and beatitude could not be complete until that event. If Calvin had been writing about Buchanan, instead of *vice versa*, he would not have forgotten the matter, for he laid great stress upon it. 'He alone,' he says, 'has made solid progress in the Gospel, who has acquired the habit of meditating continually on a blessed resurrection.' Buchanan's silence here and on other points that have been mentioned, and the scantiness, brevity, for the most part simply Theistic references he makes to matters of faith, are significant. He clearly was not zealous about most of those doctrines on which the Reforming preachers placed the greatest emphasis. His training and wide intellectual illumination must have stood in the way of his sympathising with the more violent among them, probably not excepting Knox himself occasionally. In this connection one thinks of another illustrious son of the Renaissance, Erasmus, Buchanan's senior by forty years. After all he had said and done, the Protestants demanded, with loud reproaches, that he should publicly join their ranks. Erasmus would not, perhaps could not. The alternate violence and unctuousness of the Evangelicals repelled him as much as the ignorance, and worse, of the monks disgusted him. With certain reforms in morals, constitution, and discipline, he did not see why the old Church should not be satisfactorily worked on the lines of the traditional doctrine and ritual. Probably he thought that if a man could reconcile himself to the Nicene dogmas and their consequences, it was not worth his pains boggling over Transubstantiation. Although any one may see that his heart was in many things with the Reform movement, he had never directly and openly denied any dogma. Apparently he was not prepared in his own mind to do so.

If a man is asked, 'Do you deny that Abracadabra is Mesopotamia?' he can probably say 'No' quite conscientiously; and there can be no doubt that this attitude of non-denial is widely accepted for positive faith. The Roman Church, and the Roman Empire before it, were quite willing to take it so. If a man would hold his peace, they would let him alone. Erasmus condemned the outbreak of Luther, whose faith in the immense amount of doctrine he left untouched he perhaps regarded as simply a huge faculty of taking things for granted, ending in straining at the gnat and swallowing the camel. For myself, as one of the crowd, I am glad that with all his blunders and shortcomings, so easy to point out at this distance, Luther took his own way, and did what he did. Truth is greater than peace. 'Ye shall know the truth, and the truth shall make you free,' is the method of

Christianity, unless the Founder of it is mistaken. The martyrs had faults and weaknesses—say even that they were mistaken,—but they were men of nobler spirit, and did more for us and our liberties than the *traditores,* the 'traitors' who handed over their Scriptures to the Prætor rather than face the lions. Up to a certain point, Buchanan's attitude seems to have been practically that of Erasmus. He tells us himself in his *Autobiography,* that while a student at the University of Paris (1526-29, pp. 20-23) he 'fell into the spreading flame of the Lutheran sect.' Several years later (1535-38), while resident in Scotland, he wrote some satirical verses on the Franciscan monks, which the brethren took in high dudgeon, very much to Buchanan's astonishment—boys always are astonished that frogs should object to the pleasant amusement of being stoned,—and gave him so much annoyance, ending in his having to flee the country for his life, as to make him, in his own words, 'more keenly hostile to the licentiousness of the clergy, and less indisposed to the Lutheran cause than before.'

Silent Doubt

All this time, however, he appears not to have attacked or denied anything in creed or ritual, although there cannot be a doubt that he had his own secret doubts. The relentless persecution of the monkish enemies he had made for himself at last brought him before the Inquisition (1548) at Coimbra, in Portugal, where he was acting as 'Regent' in a college recently founded by the King; but although the Inquisitors had him through their hands several times, they discovered nothing against him that could properly be called heretical. He was said to have eaten flesh in Lent, but everybody did it there, when they could get it. He was said to have given it as his opinion that on the Eucharistic controversy Augustine's opinions were more favourable to the Lutherans than to the Church; but that was merely literary or historical criticism, not heresy. Two young gentlemen testified that Buchanan was not at heart a good Catholic—which was probably true enough, but was not specific. So they shut him up, as already said, in a monastery to be taught by monks, who, though good fellows, did not know anything; and for want of something better to do, Buchanan made his famous Latin paraphrase of the Psalms. What must his Faith have been during those years? Manifestly, like that of Erasmus, less a positive assent than an abstinence from denial. Would he deny Transubstantiation or the Trinity? No, he was not ready to do anything of the kind—anyhow, not yet.

It need not be maintained that in all this Buchanan, or Erasmus either, was merely seeking to save his own skin. He may have thought that it was best for the order and edification of society to let things alone. Probably too, by this time, that spirit of Stoicism, which I have shown reason for believing sank deeper into Buchanan's nature as time went on, was beginning to assert itself. And here, in passing may I say that the common popular image of the Stoic as a gloomy, unbending, sour, cantankerous, repulsive curmudgeon, is a mistake. There is nothing in Stoicism to make him so, and as a matter of fact he was not so. Aurelius was a finished gentleman. Seneca had all the culture of his time, and was the poet of the day. Boëtius was a polished courtier. When Buchanan went over to the Reformers, it was the smartest epigrammatist going who was joining the most advanced party and leaving the 'stupid' party behind. To return. It was a well-known rule of the Stoics not to quarrel with the popular beliefs, but, if possible, to utilise them for good, as we see Buchanan does with the Pagan mythology in his Dirge on Calvin's death. Socrates, their model wise man, teaches conformity to the cult of the city where the sage resides; and everybody will recollect the care with which, as his trial approached, he arranged that Esculapius should have the cock that was due him. Probably Esculapius is still receiving a good deal of that class of poultry. For a long time—indeed until he was fifty-five, the last five of which he spent in carefully scrutinising and balancing theological controversies, and examining the whole situation—Buchanan followed the lines of Erasmus, used the cult of the Roman Esculapius to go on with, pending eventualities. But when the termination of the Guisian tyranny in Scotland made it safe for him to return, he had to make up his mind whether he was to side with the cause of oppression as advocated by the Church in which he had been born and lived up to now, or that in which, though unfortunately with certain drawbacks, a battle was being fought for liberty to express opinions different from those taught by the Church. Nobody who knew Buchanan could doubt what his choice would be.

The transition would be all the easier that in his new quarters he would find much less to offend his philosophic reason than in his old ones; but would there not be an occasional bird to be sacrificed still? He had been doing it all his Catholic life. Was it completely over now? That is not likely. But, however that may be, Buchanan was the least dogmatic and the most tolerant of all the theologically instructed men who helped to give Protestantism its place in Scotland. He might have preached had he chosen, but as he shrank from priest's orders in the Catholic Church, so he shrank in the Protestant from a position in which he would be bound to dogmatise. He did not frown upon Mary's private Mass, while Knox denounced it as worse than ten thousand armed opponents. When he narrates the hanging of a priest, according to statute, for saying Mass a third time, he does not exult, as was no doubt done by the men of the 'Congregation,' and possibly by Knox himself, when they heard of the happy event. There is nothing about him of the zeal of the renegade, who often out-Herods Herod in championing his new faith—a tendency from which Knox was by no means free. In his *History* he evidently tries to hold the balance fair between Catholic and Protestant, and is as just to Mary of Guise as to Moray. His whole religious career points to a man who thought profoundly and inquired anxiously after truth, and was careful to give expression to his feeling of reverence for the mystery of being by outward conformity with a creed and ritual to which he could more or less reconcile his reason. Well might James Melville (Rev., not Sir) describe him not only as a 'maist learned and wyse,' but also as a 'maist godlie' man, although he himself might have preferred 'spiritual' as a more comprehensive epithet.

It may be objected that men like Buchanan and Erasmus did not act honestly in remaining silent and conforming members of a system which they secretly regarded as in many vital respects false, and an imposture upon the world. Of course, it is to be said for Buchanan that he did ultimately come out of it; but then, why not sooner? Why did he not earlier follow the lead of Luther and Calvin and Knox? For one thing, it must be remembered that even these great heroes of veracity had probably their reticences. At all events, they have left to us the legacy of an incompletely performed work. Was their outspokenness equal to Christ's? His brought Him to the cross. It seems to be in the nature of the Ideal that to make an utterly clean breast of it should be perilous or fatal to its revealer, and the hero of Truth who dies in his bed has probably made a good many compromises with his conscience to achieve that result. It is all a matter of degree, a comparison of the well and the very well, of the bad and the too bad. A good man is a man who tries to be good, and a bad man is a man who does not care whether he is bad or good. But man is finite, and there can be nothing absolute in human life, except perhaps the absolute fool who thinks there may. Everything depends on the state of the facts. In these days, for instance, when historical and speculative criticism has put Scripture and the supernatural in so very different a position from that assigned to them by the Reformers, there is too good reason to believe, especially in the light of intra-ecclesiastical demands for the revision of Confessions and Articles, that many of the clergy feel extremely uneasy in being pledged to dogmas which they more or less disbelieve. As they could not speak out without having to face starvation for those dependent on them, a merciful man might be disposed to say that while the situation was bad, it was perhaps not unpardonable, and that the person implicated might still be regarded as a good and otherwise honestly intentioned man. But if the inner state of mind should be one of hopeless antagonism to the supernatural, one would be disposed to say that it was 'too bad' to remain, and that speaking out and coming out, at any cost, was the duty of the position.

Bearing in mind that Buchanan carried his life in his hand, and that he had never undertaken the function of religious teacher, only a very heroic person could afford to say that he had not done all he dared, and that he showed himself deeply in earnest about Truth, when at last he had the opportunity, and really 'was of gud religion for a poet,' and even for a more hopeful character. Buchanan, on the intellectual side of him, was not merely a poet, but a wit and humorist—a type of mind not in itself easy to harmonise with being of 'gud religion.' Perhaps if the Puritans had not been in so many cases hopelessly wooden, it might have saved their cause from having so many joints in its harness open to the shafts of the satirical sharpshooter, but they would probably not have done so great and grave a work in the world. Dire, however, are the fruits of an igneous temperament and a ligneous intellect, and Praise-God Barebones and Co. have done an evil turn to a good undertaking. The capacity and habit of seeing and enjoying the ludicrous are a temptation to their possessor to forget that life has its serious aspect also, and in too many instances this seems to be forgotten. Hence the presumption is against the laugher until he has become better known. I recollect once hearing a celebrated preacher give a highly comical account of his own conversion, and albeit not given to the frowning mood, I could not help asking myself whether this could be a serious man; and it was not until I read his life that I saw he knew that there is a time for everything under the sun, and that he possessed the secret of assigning its due claim to all views of life. Buchanan, too, had mastered this power—for it requires an effort of will, and there must always be an essential difference between the humorous man's view of religion, and that of the man who cannot show his teeth by way of smile, though Nestor swear the jest be laughable. Buchanan could sparkle when sparkling was in place, but he could also be depended on when grave or even grim work was in request.

Renaissance Morals

Part of the price paid for the enlightenment of the Renaissance was that in too many instances its breadth of ethical as well as intellectual outlook was allowed by its possessor to sink into a practical licentiousness, open or concealed, that corrupted, or even totally destroyed, the moral and spiritual faculties. I cannot see proof of any such results in Buchanan's case. I think he was careful to secure himself from danger on this side of his temptations. His bitterest detractors do not raise a whisper against him here. But there is a section of his poetry which may best be characterised as of the *Ad Neæram, In Leonoram (Lenam), Ad Gelliam, Ad Briandum Vallium pro Lena Apologia* order, which has occasioned misgiving to some of his friends. One biographer, a very competent authority on this period of Scottish history, says, somewhat severely, that these pieces ought not to have been written by the man who wrote *Franciscanus*—a powerful satire on the vices and hypocrisy of the monks. I must say that, with every deference to a critic highly worthy of respect, I am not able to see it. The *Franciscanus* was essentially an exposure of dishonesty, not so much of the vices practised under the cowl, as of the shameful trickery of using the cowl to cloak them. As far as honesty and consistency go, there is no reason why an honest and consistent man should not have written every word of these 'Lena' sketches. Even from an artistic point of view they will stand inspection. The subject, of course, is a revolting one, and so is Dame Quickly—but would any man of average robustness of mind wish Dame Quickly unwritten? Many people seem to forget that while the real itself may be unpleasant, the artistic image of the real may be a delight. We should shrink from Caliban in the flesh, but Shakespeare throws a charm over him; Pandemonium is not, I believe, a sweet scene, but Milton's account of it is sublime; Falstaff was disreputable, but he makes an admirable stage figure; a corpse is an unlovely object, but Rembrandt's 'Dissectors' has a fascination.

Probably it was for want of noting this distinction that the late Principal Shairp, who was a good judge of a certain class of poetry, lamented that Burns should have written *Holy Willie's Prayer* and the *Jolly Beggars*!—a remark which led Louis Stevenson, in a compassionating way, to hint that Burns was perhaps too 'burly' a figure for the Principal's microscope. There is a good deal of this 'burliness' in Buchanan's *Leonoras*, which in point of graphic power are second only to the *Jolly Beggars*, while their savage and even hideous realism, contrasting with the elegance of the Latin line, produce a piquant effect from the mere point of view of art. But I demur to any suggestion that these or any of Buchanan's so-called 'amorous' poetry are corrupting or intended to be, or that they exhibit any gloating over the degrading or the degraded on the part of the writer. From references in them I believe they were satires written for the warning of 'college' youth, and resembled certain passages in the Book of Proverbs and elsewhere in the Bible, where certain counsels, highly necessary and practical, are conveyed in language not deficient either in directness or detail. They could not possibly scandalise or tempt any one, being written in Latin. Mr. Podsnap and the 'young person' would pass equally scatheless, for they could not read them. Only men who could construe and scan Horace could understand them, and these might be trusted to see their true drift. Then the *Ad Gelliam* verses were merely playful little satires upon ladies who painted, or wore brass rings and glass gems, which might amuse readers, while producing no effect, good or evil, upon their subjects. As to the *Neæra* series, they are not love-poems at all, but epigrams. There is no passion, sensuous or otherwise, in them. What show of manufactured emotion there may be is simply a stage-scaffolding on which to plant and fire off the epigram. Probably the best known of the series is the following:—

'Illa mihi semper præsenti dura Neæra,
Me quoties absum semper abesse dolet;
Non desiderio nostri, non mœret amore,
Sed se non nostro posse dolore frui';

which James Hannay, who was well able to appreciate this class of work, translated thus:—

'Neæra is harsh at our every greeting,
Whene'er I am absent, she wants me again;
'Tis not that she loves me, or cares for our meeting,
She misses the pleasure of seeing my pain';

adding that 'Ménage used to say that he would have given his best benefice to have written the lines—and Ménage held some fat ones.' What anchorite could discover anything exceptionable here, or if he had any intelligence left, could fail to perceive that it was simply a case for admiring extreme cleverness of thought and smartness of phrase? If any one desires to see how Buchanan could appreciate and address the highest type of womanhood, let him read such verses as the *Ad Mildredam* or the *Ad Camillam Morelliam*, and he will see that he was a man with tenderness in him as well as virility, with grace as well as severity of speech; and the fact that in his maturer years he was not ashamed to publish the incriminated poetry, showed that he was not conscious of anything to be ashamed of, that he knew the poet's dominion was conterminous with the whole range of things, and no part of it whatever exempt from his critical or sympathetic function, while his fiercest or lightest dealing with the facts of life is in no way inconsistent with a profound and silent veneration in presence of the mystery of existence.

CHAPTER VI
BIOGRAPHICAL FACTS

Earlier and Continental

Buchanan was born early in February 1506, at Moss or Mid-Leowen, on the Blane Water, about two miles south-east of Killearn in Stirlingshire, of a 'family ancient rather than opulent,' as he tells us in his *Autobiography*, so that he was delivered from the peasant or upstart consciousness which, except in the priesthood, would, in those feudal times, have handicapped him heavily in the race of life. His real and Scoto-Irish clan name was Macauslan, but the Macauslan having acquired the lands of Buchanan in the Lennox, took the name of his property, and became Buchanan of that Ilk; and thus it came to pass that our George ranked as a 'cadet of Buchanan,' as Hannay was proud and particular to specify. Ancient lineage, however, is no insurance against misfortune, and the Buchanans of Moss, never rich, sank into deep poverty. The father died in George's youth, and the grandfather who survived him was a waster and became a bankrupt, and Agnes Heriot, the mother, was left to struggle with the upbringing of five sons and three daughters—a task however, which she successfully accomplished, like the heroine she was, as her most distinguished son gratefully commemorates. Having never known wealth or luxury, perhaps it was easier for Buchanan to reconcile himself to their opposites in after years. In the Lennox they talked Gaelic, and Buchanan picked up that speech to begin with. He would also learn some Scotch or Northern English from his mother, who came from Haddingtonshire, and in addition she was careful to have him sent to the schools in the neighbourhood, where he could learn the elements of Latin.

For the old Church had not entirely neglected popular education, as has been shown, in a very interesting way, in Grant's *Burgh Schools of Scotland*, and as, indeed, appears on the face of the Reformers' *First Book of Discipline* itself (1560). Most of the burghs maintained schools, both secondary and elementary, so that the barons and freeholders who were ordered by the celebrated Act of James IV. (1494) to keep their heirs at school until they had learned 'perfyt Latyn'—then the international language of the educated and of diplomacy—had abundant opportunity of doing so had they chosen, although unfortunately they too seldom chose; so that the burgh schools were largely recruiting-grounds for the priesthood. There were also elementary Church schools, in many cases taught by women, and private adventure schools; and in these a considerable number of the children of the poor were taught at least to read. Accordingly, when it is said that Knox and the Reformers established the Scottish Parish School system, a little discrimination must be exercised. They did not invent popular education—they found it; but they did invent, on paper, in the *First Book of Discipline*, the idea of bringing education to the people's doors, by securing that there should be a school wherever there was a 'kirk'—that is, practically in every parish; so that 'the youth-head and tender children shall be nourished and brought up in vertue, *in presence of their friends*, by whose good attendance many inconveniences may be avoyded in which the youth commonly fall, either by over much libertie which they have in strange and unknowne places, while they cannot rule themselves; or else for lack of good attendance, and of such necessaries as their tender age requires.'

So far the *Book of Discipline*, at once recognising an existing educational system, and suggesting, for reason given, the vital improvement of its national application! The whole scheme, indeed, is admirable, including as it does compulsion, the picking out and, in the case of the poor, supporting the class of youth suited for the higher kinds of service to society, while the others not so gifted 'must be set to some handie craft, or to some other profitable exercise'—that is, technical education, or some other form of practical training. I have said 'on paper,' but not by way of sneer, and ought to add in passing, that it was not the fault of Knox and his associates that it remained to a great extent merely 'on paper,' instead of being immediately and effectually established. It was the fault and the disgrace of a different type of men. Knox, as I have already said, was a politician, and made dexterous use of the 'Lords of the Congregation' to secure the triumph of Protestantism. But these 'Lords of the Congregation' were politicians also, and made an equally dexterous use of Knox to fill their own pockets with Church spoil—I except a few, who were really noble men. They gave little for parish churches, and nothing that I ever heard of for parish schools. The whole thing broke poor Knox's heart. It did not ruffle Buchanan, although he was probably the greatest educational enthusiast in Europe at the moment. But he was really a greater intelligence and a calmer master of himself than Knox, and probably knew that any one who expects to find more than twenty-five per cent.—if so much—of the race as existing at any given moment worthy of intellectual or moral respect, must either have had little experience of life, or possess a very low standard of human excellence.

Not till 1696 was the plan of the *Book of Discipline* adumbrated in legislation, and the successors of the 'Lords of the Congregation' bound by law to provide a school-house and a salaried teacher in every parish. But during the whole of the intervening century and a third, the Presbyterian clergy never ceased in their efforts, and often their sacrifices, for popular education, while at the same time fighting a steady battle for liberty against as mean and cruel a crusade of Absolutist Monarchy and Ecclesiastical Tyranny as ever was preached by a ridiculous and pedant Peter against a self-respecting people. For myself, I fail to find much of the theology of the Covenanters credible—although I must say I should like if we could hear Knox and Melville, or even Cameron and Cargill, on the existing state of things. I think we should get some different guidance from what we are receiving from those blind leaders of the blind who shiveringly and stammeringly attempt to fill their places. For it is almost impossible to appraise too highly the service done by the Covenanters for the cause of liberty and popular education; and although they had their very obvious faults, one is always sorry to think that the aristocratic and Episcopalian prejudices of Scott should have led him to hold them up to ridicule, while glad that a higher and juster view was taken by a greater Scotsman even than Scott, when, in answer to a contemptuous critic of the men of the Covenant, Burns turned on him with the withering *impromptu*:—

> 'The Solemn League and Covenant
> Cost Scotland blood—cost Scotland tears—
> But it sealed Freedom's sacred cause—
> If thou'rt a slave, indulge thy sneers.'[5]

We go back to young George Buchanan (1517-19) at the Catholic local grammar-school of Killearn or Dumbarton, or wherever else in the neighbourhood secondary education was to be had. The boy had shown such aptitude that his uncle, James Heriot, who is said to have been Justiciar of Lothian, sent him to the University of Paris, then, though not quite so much as at an earlier date, enjoying the reputation of the most notable of any seat of learning in existence. Instead of being required to pass through the preparatory school, he at once began his studies in the Arts faculty (1520, age fourteen), his Scottish acquirements having apparently been sufficient to pass him through whatever entrance examination was imperative. Here he spent about two years, working mainly at Latin versification, which, as his reputation for Latin poetry was to be the making of him in after years, was perhaps the best thing he could do, especially as he liked it. At this point, as evil fate would have it, his uncle died, and he himself fell ill. But as he was penniless, he had to struggle home, illness and all, as best he could, and was not able to move about again for a year or thereabouts (1523). And then it turned out that a very singular purpose had entered the mind of the ill or convalescent student of seventeen.

[Here ends Dr. Wallace's MS.]

That purpose was to enlist as a volunteer in an army for the invasion of England, to be led by the Regent Albany, who had supposed wrongs of his own as well as of the borders to avenge against that old neighbour and untiring enemy. That army, consisting of French auxiliaries and Scottish recruits, marched to Melrose and then partly crossed the Tweed by a wooden bridge, then, holding Flodden in memory, intimated a mutinous resolution not to cross the border, then marched down the left bank of the river, and for three days besieged Wark Castle to little effect, then made a sudden night-march to Lauder in a snowstorm, 'which told heavily on man and beast,' and reduced Buchanan to very bad health for the rest of the winter. Buchanan, when he came to write his own life in his old age, had come to believe that he joined this abortive expedition to learn the art of war, which, without intentions more far-seeing than those of a lad of eighteen, he certainly did, just as Gibbon was educated to understand the evolution of the phalanx and the legions, by what he saw, in his two and a half years' captaincy of the Hampshire Militia, of the evolutions of a modern battalion. In the spring of 1525 Buchanan appeared as a 'pauper student' at the University of St. Andrews, doubtless specially well qualified both as a student and as a 'pauper'—which epithet 'pauper,' however, meant probably nothing more opprobrious than a youth who required board and education free, like many a score of St. Andrews students, from poet Buchanan to poet Fergusson, who about two and a half centuries later sat at the bursar's free table and said grace over the too plentiful college rabbits that were last century procured from the links that now swarm only with golfers. He was sent there, he tells in his *Autobiography,* to 'sit at the feet of John Major,' the celebrated logician of that age; but he did not long sit at his feet as pupil before he felt in a position to criticise his master as a teacher of sophistry rather than logic. Next summer, having taken the St. Andrews B.A. degree, he followed or accompanied Major to Paris, and there passed through two years' adversity under pressure of poverty and the suspicion of not being an orthodox Papist. Fortune relaxed her frown, and he was admitted to the College of Ste. Barbe, in which he was Professor of Grammar for three years. Meanwhile Gilbert Kennedy, the young Earl of Cassilis, one of the earliest of Scottish hero-worshippers, had the insight to appreciate his learning and genius, and the devotion to adhere to him as friend, pupil, and protector for five years. In 1533, the tutor dedicated to the pupil his translation of Linacre's Grammar, one of the items of work done by him during his professorship in the College of Ste. Barbe; and in 1558, after this pupil, who had held a prominent position among Scottish nobles, died, probably from poison, at Dieppe, on his way home from the marriage of Mary Stuart to the Dauphin, along with the other three Scottish commissioners who had attended it, Buchanan celebrated him in emphatic Latin verse that is now better known than most contemporary epitaphs. Let it be told, however, to illustrate the cross-threads that run through the web of life, that Queen Mary, on 9th October 1564, granted to Buchanan, who had been her tutor also, and probably the most learned and intellectual of all her friends, a pension of £500 Scots, or £25 sterling a year, from the Abbey of Crossraguel; that the then Earl of Cassilis, son of Buchanan's old pupil, claimed the temporalities of that abbey as his own, and sometimes stopped temporarily, and often permanently diminished, the pension which had been granted by the Queen out of the spoils of the Reformation, tarnishing by pious Protestant greed the brightest page in the history of the earldom of Cassilis.

After Buchanan's tutorship of the father of this grasping Protestant was ended, and Buchanan was proposing to return to his old scholar's life in Paris, James V. detained him to act as tutor to one of his natural sons—not the one known afterwards as the Good Regent, but James Stewart, Prior of Coldingham. This king, who entertained the idea that the clergy ought not to disregard the moral law as if they were royal personages like himself, set Buchanan to the not uncongenial task, upon which Dunbar and Sir David Lindsay of the Mount had previously been engaged, of 'lashing the vices' of the clergy, and especially of the monks. In the form of a dream, *Somnium*, he represented to St. Francis the reasons of a decent man for refusing to enter this order of sainthood—reasons which, because of their truth, might satisfy a saint, but which also, because of their truth, would likely be disagreeable to sanctified hypocrites and scoundrels. Two palinodes, wearing the aspect of apologies, were seen by those who understood irony to be rather stinging aggravations of the original satire. After some months of a mixed tumult of priestly rage and secular laughter, the royal love of fun and of virtue again prompted Buchanan to renew the attack, which he did by beginning *Franciscanus*, not published till 1560, and then dedicated to the Regent Moray and gradually extended to a thousand Latin lines, which contain the most polished, skilfully contemptuous exposure of the arts, ignorance, and vices of the later generations of the Romish clergy in Scotland. It is still worth reading by all who enjoy rough, boisterous, coarse humour, as also by all anti-Papist fanatics, even if they should renew their Latin studies for nine months to enable them to understand and utilise it. These men, drenched with satire, published and unpublished, whose craft of various hues was endangered by it, of course thought that it would be judicious if not just to burn its author. Cardinal Beaton had him on his list of heretics,— for what heresy could be so dangerous as disbelief in the solid, well-fed, red-faced exponents of infallible truth? In 1539 he escaped from prison in Edinburgh[6] when his guards were asleep. But being warned after the King had received the MS. of *The Franciscan* that Beaton had offered this fickle monarch a price for his head, he felt constrained to bid farewell once more to his native country. He fled to England, but, as Henry VIII. was then busy burning all shades of believers that did not suit his personal fancy, Buchanan thought it prudent to trust his safety and his fortunes once more to Paris. On arriving there, however, he found that Cardinal Beaton was there before him as ambassador, so on the invitation of Andrew Gouvéa he withdrew to Bordeaux. There he taught three years at least in the public schools, and wrote four tragedies for the annual exhibitions of these schools, to wit *The Baptist, Medea, Jepthes,* and *Alcestis.* In the College of Guyenne he had Gouvéa as a principal, and as a pupil Montaigne, the celebrated sceptic, who is dogmatic enough to state in one of his essays that Gouvéa was 'without comparison the chiefest rector in France,' and that he himself had, as a principal actor, 'undergone and represented the chiefest parts in the Latin Tragedies of Buchanan.' When here, Beaton and the Franciscans harassed him until that fear was dispelled by the plague raging over Aquitaine and the death of his fickle patron, the King of Scots.

Next, about 1547, in the wake or under the convoy of Gouvéa, he migrated to Portugal in response to the invitation of the King to teach in a resuscitation of the University of Coimbra that was being then worked out at great expense for education in the liberal arts and the philosophy of Aristotle. Many of his friends, eminent for learning, were there before him, and he expected to find peace in that out of the way corner of the world. But Gouvéa died suddenly, and then all his enemies ran at him with open mouth. He was thrown into prison, charged with writing against the Franciscans and eating flesh in Lent. The Inquisitors tormented themselves and him for six months without stateable result; and then, thinking it prudent, and perhaps honest, to conceal that their toil had been in vain, they shut him up in a monastery to be converted to the true faith or to be prepared for the fagots. To the great scholar, however, the monks, though ignorant, behaved not unkindly. They allowed him the truest literary leisure and quiet he ever had except perhaps in St. Andrews; and he devoted it to the so-called translation of David's Psalms into Latin verse, which are in truth artistic evolutionary expositions from Hebrew hints, or splendid blossoms of sacred poetry grown from the seed given by the poet-king of

Israel to the winds of heaven, in the moments of inspiration occurring in a life of suffering, of passion, and of hope. Never elsewhere did the iron fetters of Buchanan's own environment permit him to soar so close to the firmament.

When set at liberty, though the King of Portugal offered him the means of subsistence, he returned to England. But as affairs were then in disorder under a young king, he in a short time returned to France and celebrated the siege of Metz in a Latin poem, not without the approbation which rewarded all his efforts in that line of composition. Thereafter the Marshal de Brissac called him to Italy, and he lived with him and his son in Italy and France for four years till 1560, spending much time in writing his poem *De Sphæra*, and in study of the religious controversies then seething through civilised Europe, and carrying it into a scientific region that rendered a poetic exposition of the Ptolemaic system a work of futility and utterly misspent power.

In 1561 he returned to his native country, and there indicated his Rationalistic leanings to the side of Protestantism. Nevertheless, the non-Protestant Mary Stuart, of ever-living memory in the realm of history and romance, pursued her studies in Livy and other classics with his help. As formerly mentioned, she endowed him with a pension of £500 a year. But in after years Mary's faults or her misfortunes threw them into the hostile camps that tore Scotland into confusion and deadly discord. In regard to the murder of Darnley, he came to the conclusion, on the evidence of open foes and of professed friends, that she was guilty. He preferred truth to the beautiful queen, and it is difficult to comprehend how any man capable of weighing and scrutinising such evidence as was accessible to him can blame him.[7]

Buchanan has been accused of ingratitude to Mary, his friend as well as his mistress, divinely gifted and divinely appointed. He may have been compelled to seem ungrateful through the lying of ill-informed Reformers and rogues; but sure am I that his Latin and other Humanist studies with that most fascinating and accomplished of women, or at least of queens, gave him the opportunity of forming an idea of her intellectual powers and unsurpassed personal charms that no other contemporary in Scotland was mentally and morally capable of forming, and I don't doubt that this idea finds sincere expression in his dedication to her of his version or paraphrase of the Psalms of the Hebrew poet-king, without any hint whatever of kindred royal frailties, or of tendencies thereto. What Buchanan must have seen in her when he had the best opportunity of sight and knowledge stands recorded unalterably in his noble verse that rolls down the centuries, bearing an impress of insight and sincerity unequalled in the poetical portraiture of queens till Tennyson laid his dedication at the feet of the most illustrious and fortunate of all her countless descendants. A true poet I believe to be a true seer, and incapable of falsehood to the extent that he has had the chance to see. But a true poet may be deceived. Spenser and Shakespeare were deceived into uttering gross flatteries about Queen Elizabeth; but they were deceived by the dense atmosphere of lying by which one of the cleverest, falsest, most hateful of women of all history encompassed herself. That Queen Mary should have been no worse than she was in a world with her royal cousin and rival flaunting her fictitious moral and physical beauties at the head of it, and getting prematurely canonised as the Good Queen Bess, ought certainly to qualify or blot out for ever all that can be stated truly and justly in condemnation or even grave censure of Queen Mary. Therefore let the modest and honest muse of History cease howling and canting about her crimes, and try to refrain from lavishing eulogy upon her kindred in position and in blood—Henry VIII., the Royal Bluebeard, and his inconstant, cruel, deceitful daughter—a pair of monarchs whose fickle affections led so many adventurous wives and ambitious wooers to the scaffold, by processes that involved the partial but temporary corruption of their country's conscience.

The wants and troubles of his country beset Buchanan with many a call of duty, and cast upon him loads of multifarious work, such as perhaps never in the history of human-kind before were thrown upon the most accomplished and studious of living men. The tasks assigned to Buchanan, and the duties imposed upon him, reflect no inconsiderable honour and credit upon his lawless, homicidal, half-civilised countrymen. While still friendly with Queen Mary, he gave effect to his Reformation convictions, by sitting and working for years, from 1563 onwards, as a member of the new-born democratic General Assembly, knowing well enough that it was an institution that the Queen would have been happy to see strangled, even before it began to discuss the scandals of Rizzio and Darnley with the plain-spoken impudence of a rustic kirk-session and the arrogance of an infallible tribunal. Buchanan was one of the Commissioners that revised the *Book of Discipline*, and, along with Knox and others, was a member of a committee appointed to confer regarding the causes that fell, or that ought to fall, within the jurisdiction of the Kirk. In 1567, a few days after the beginning of Mary's imprisonment in Lochleven, Buchanan filled the chair of the Moderator of the General Assembly, a position that for generations has not called for the worldly wisdom and terse, impatient talk of a layman, and seldom, if ever, so much required to be reminded of the limits of its power and jurisdiction as when Buchanan sat as its Moderator, and the head of the State was a captive.

In the previous year, Queen Mary's half-brother, the Earl of Moray, commendator of the Priory of St. Andrews, and as such patron of the Principalship of St. Leonard's College there, appointed Buchanan to that office, which he held for four years. During these years St. Leonard's, which in the first year was studentless, became the best attended of the three St. Andrews colleges. But the fame of the 'greatest poet of the age' could not permanently revive the fortunes of St. Leonard's, nor did the efforts of the Parliamentary Commission of 1579, of which Andrew Melville as well as Buchanan were members. By the time Dr. Johnson was on his way to the Hebrides, the College buildings were ruinous and forsaken, including St. Leonard's Church, of which the Doctor could not see the inside, because of decent excuses exciting in his mind the hope that 'Where there is still shame there may yet be virtue.'[8]

The Regent Moray, Buchanan's patron and friend, to whom the *Franciscanus* was dedicated, was a recognised mainstay of Protestantism, heartily hated by the allies of the Queen and of the Pope. He was assassinated in Linlithgow on 20th January 1570, partly to further their interests and partly to gratify private revenge. Hamilton of Bothwellhaugh was waiting for him in the house of his uncle, Archbishop Hamilton, with small-bore matchlock and lighted match, and the accident of a crowded street gave him the opportunity of a deliberate aim. His death was laid at the door of the Hamiltons, and it stirred the patriotism of Buchanan to write a political pamphlet, called an *Admonition to the Trew Lordes*, in the vernacular of Scotland, directed against the Hamiltons and their friends—a publication full of practical insight, good sense, and cogent argument, the work of a wise, earnest, sagacious man, who in the zeal for the good of his country forgot that he had the gift of poetic inspiration, in that respect very unlike his great successor Milton when he too became a political pamphleteer, more rhapsodical than relevant. He suspected the Hamiltons of a desire to secure the crown, and Buchanan very much preferred to them Queen Mary and her son, whose birth he had welcomed as a star of hope for his country. His birthday ode of welcome, ostensibly intended for the boy when he grew up, but positively in the meantime for the guidance and the warning of his mother, is in substance a serious homily on the duty of kings to God and the people, from whom their power came, and whose will and welfare alone justified its exercise. The essence of the *De Jure Regni* underlies it, an essence never practically intelligible to the fated House of Stuart. Neither the beautiful, brilliant Mary nor her erratic but not stupid race could understand the teaching of Buchanan as an exposition of the law of the King of kings. The fate of that race, from her flight to England to the flight from Culloden, has helped the world to understand it. They were doomed to be born in and live through ages of ignorance, superstition, and falsehood, in which few men arose who could discover and recognise truth and publish it at their risk for the dark here and the darker hereafter, as was done by Buchanan. He may not have been infallible, but he had insight, veracity, and courage, the like of which will never be exhibited by his traducers to the end of time. Those who can believe him guilty of base ingratitude and malicious falsehood are incapable of discriminating the best from the worst in human nature and in human history.

Buchanan's truthfulness and resolute desire to be impartial can be best inferred in our time from his *History of Scotland*, at which he had written for years, and for which he had collected materials from his boyhood. The style of it appears to be an eclectic adaptation of available and appropriate elements from the styles of Livy, Sallust, and Tacitus. It wants the special charm of 'Livy's pictured page,' for Scottish places, deeds, heroes, and tastes did not for Buchanan's earnest, realistic, dialectical, judicial mind present inducements to poetic word-painting—indeed, it was after his day, before the fascinations of the picturesque dawned upon the mind of Scotland, unless it may have been to some semi-mythical, mist-inspired member of the tribe of Ossian. The speeches of his *History* are the most tersely expressed, forcibly reasoned specimens of ancient Scottish oratory, assuming, of course, that they ought to have been delivered, but that they never were. They want the terse, pregnant suggestiveness of the orations of Tacitus; but they may probably appear to be not less skilfully adapted for the dramatic surroundings in which they are supposed to have been delivered. Young students of Latin, especially in the Aberdeen region, have found it to be for their interest to read and re-read Buchanan's *History*, and it is in the original that the literary art and linguistic skill of its author can be best seen. But it is still worth reading, and is often read in Dr. Watkins' translation, which as a translation reflects a good deal more credit upon its author than his old-womanly, newspapery but not dishonest attempt at original historical composition shown in his bringing down of Buchanan's masterly story to the culmination or extinction of Scottish history in the visit of George IV. to Edinburgh. The babes and sucklings of the school of Dry-as-dust assert that Buchanan is superseded as an historian; but a man of Buchanan's powers and opportunities can never be superseded as a narrator of the history of his own time.

Buchanan died on the 28th September 1582, a few days or weeks after his *History* had been published. He had striven, in spite of old age, ill-health, and poverty, to accomplish this long-meditated patriotic task; and when he had corrected the proofs and given it to the world, he felt that his last slender tie to life was broken, and his long, chequered, poorly-paid day's work was done.

His death took place in Kennedy's Close, the second close off the High Street of Edinburgh above the Tron Church, as recorded by 'George Paton, Antiquary,' upon the rather reliable authority of an ancient Lord Advocate, Sir James Stewart of Goodtrees.

His last lodging was in 'the first house in the turnpike above the tavern,' and occupied some few cubic feet of space, probably about twelve feet above the existing causeway blocks of Hunter Square, an entirely vanished pile of tall, substantial, over-populated masonry, part of the crest of the High Street once, standing within a quarter of a mile of the vanished garden in which Darnley was found dead in his shirt without mark of violence, still nearer to the site of the vanished house in which Walter Scott was born, and to the vacant air-space once filled by Johnny Dowie's vanished tavern, in which during his Edinburgh sojourn Robert Burns was wont to make merry with select friends.

The records of the Commissary Court show that Buchanan left no property except £100 of his Crossraguel pension (gifted by Queen Mary, and withheld as often and as long as he could by the Earl of Cassilis), which had been in arrear from the previous Whitsunday. His 'Inventar' exhibits him in his true character of an ancient philosopher, whether Stoic or not. The civic authorities of Edinburgh, who from time immemorial have been ready and willing to bury scholars, buried his body the day after his death at the public expense. The ground of Greyfriars, one of the spoils of the Reformation, was then being turned into a burying-ground, and Buchanan was the 'first person of celebrity' buried in it. The exact spot of his sepulture is, however, in doubt, though a small tablet was put up by a humble blacksmith to mark where it is believed to be—a tribute of hero-worship like to that in Parliament Square which is supposed to mark the burial-place of Knox.

It is not likely that Buchanan ever asked the Town Council of Edinburgh for bread, but it is believed that they gave him a stone—without any inscription, however, to show for whom it was intended, so that by 1701 it was lost or stolen. His skull also is believed to be one of the lawful and sacred possessions of the Edinburgh University. If genuine, it may be a phrenological curiosity. Sir W. Hamilton once used it at a lecture which was listened to and approved of by Thomas Carlyle. Sir William demonstrated to Carlyle's satisfaction that the said skull, supposed to be Buchanan's, was according to phrenological dogmas far inferior to that of some 'Malay cut-throat' or other unredeemed ruffian. Assuming this to be the fact—and my authority for believing it is a letter of Carlyle published in Veitch's *Life* of Sir W. Hamilton—I am surprised that Mr. Hosack and Sir John Skelton were not converted to phrenology. But for my part, believing in the universal but mostly untranslatable symbolism of Nature, from the 'flower in the crannied wall' to the human face and form divine, and believing only to a limited extent in phrenology as the dark side of physiognomy that is open to touch rather than to sight, I should hold that the skull which was inferior to a Malay's in any respect except thickness could never be the skull of Buchanan; and it would not alter my conviction to feel sure that George Combe was present at Sir William Hamilton's lecture, and for the first and only time in their career of phrenological disputation expressly agreed with him. Whatever Buchanan's head and face may have been like—and his portraits impute to him either sleepy, benevolent dulness, or ferrety, peevish conceit—it is not believable that his head or face could have ever resembled that of a Malay or any other kind of savage. So acute a logician as Sir W. Hamilton ought to have doubted one of his premises at least, and been able to conceive it possible that the resetters of dead men's skulls may be sometimes the victims of outside, as well as inside, deception.

EPILOGISTIC

The sudden and untimely death of Dr. Wallace has left this volume incomplete, and incapable of being completed as he would have done it. Detailed facts are in part awanting, but they are awanting in every biography and autobiography, and after the oblivion of centuries has passed over them, they tend to be unintelligible and uninteresting as lying remote from everyday experience. These, however, the inquiring reader, to his reasonable satisfaction, can find elsewhere; what he will never find elsewhere are Dr. Wallace's ultimate, deliberate, critical estimates of the life and work of Buchanan. His book, as it grew under his nimble pen, grew, probably unconsciously, to be not so much an articulation of the bare bones of fact as a narrative of the genesis, evolution, growth, and vitality of Buchanan's ideas, more especially his ideas affecting social democratic development, and in particular his capital heresy, dangerous for himself, but vital for the race, touching the 'rights of man.'

Few men of any country have had such versatility of talent, and have in life found tasks so varied as George Buchanan and Robert Wallace. No other Scotsman known to me, through credible report or in the flesh, has had the personal experience that would enable him so well to understand and interpret the personal experience of George Buchanan. Both were pre-eminent in the university learning of their respective eras, which had little in common except Latin; scholastic logic and metaphysic being the dominating study of Buchanan's days, as inductive positive science is of ours. Both were wandering scholars seeking for fortune, or at least for bread; each acting as tutor, schoolmaster, university professor, man of letters, theologian, politician, and teacher of public men who were too ignorant or too neglectful of honest rational principle to be fit to rule in mercy and in justice; both were doomed by circumstances or by conscience to poverty and the discrediting influences of poverty, though fit to furnish invaluable light and guidance to their fellow-men. Methinks the pre-Reformation church was a kinder, less harsh nursing-mother to the inquiring, doubting, hesitating, satirical Protestant, than the dry-as-dust nurses of ultra-Protestantism, agnosticism, atheism, and sincere worship of nothing except Mammon's golden calf were to the learned literary man of our day who, afflicted with distracting doubts himself, and many sorrows, could still give reasons for his faith in a supreme Creator and an administrator of the universe according to fixed law and unswerving right, and could help to lift the mind of his age out of a darkness deeper than Popery—the blackness of atheistic despair. Both knew about politics as revealed in the wrangling of churches or religious sects, and the strife of factions intriguing and fighting for power to govern or to misgovern. The politics familiar to Buchanan included the ethics that prompted and the arts that effected the murders of Cardinal Beaton, Rizzio, Darnley, Regent Moray, and Queen Mary, and that often imperilled his own life. Nevertheless, worn out by his years and assiduous labours, he died in his bed when his work was done, a fortnight after his *History* of his country was published, and before his old pupil the Scottish Solomon had time to discover all the treason it contained; ordered his servant to give his few last coins to a beggar, and left the care of his funeral to all whom it might concern on Christian, natural, civic, and sanitary grounds, ending his long, busy, chequered tenure of time with that courage and hope which gilds the last sunset of those who have striven to do right and never doubted that God is just.

There was no man in Scotland or in Europe that could have been of so much service to Scotland in guiding it through the troubles and storms, political, moral, and religious, of the Reformation as Buchanan, if the people of Scotland, more especially the feudal lords of Scotland, had been fit to follow the dictates of the broadest, most complete worldly wisdom, and of the clear conscience of one who had spent his years in study and in poverty, who had lived the life of a stranger to the entanglements of foolish pleasure and the illusions of earthly hope, who had the most of his possible life behind him and eternity in no distant prospect, and who had no conceivable motive to applaud murder or to tell lies. Sceptical by innate constitution, and educated to doubt in the schools of adversity and experience, personal and historical, he was not the man to commit himself hastily to faith in dark dogmas and half-explored truths; he was the man to be a cautious, judicious reformer, not the man to be an impetuous, frantic destroyer, too rash and unrestrained to discriminate between the entirely and partially unsound, too just to plunder churchmen, some of them profligate, in order to enrich feudal lords skilled in few arts except the arts of war and theft. Like Erasmus and Beza, he saw that the old order of society was dissolving; but, like all wise men, he preferred slow and gradual to revolutionary change.

John Knox, in point of culture and of pure intellect and reason, was a small man—a rash, daring, half-educated schoolboy, compared with Buchanan. Knowledge and reason are conservative forces, and Knox could not have been great had he not been a destroyer. His most indelible historical records are the ruins of cathedrals and other religious houses, 'rooks' nests' requiring to be pulled down only in the judgment of blind superstition and rabid fanaticism. For the ignorance and savagery of the people of Scotland the Church of Rome was primarily to blame. That Church required reformation, moral and intellectual; but no spiritual entity, however corrupt, can be miraculously reformed by the destruction of Gothic or any other architecture which took its form under the sincere art and piety of buried generations. Cardinal Beaton's mode of burning good true men to support and preserve the divine truth that had vitalised his Church for centuries was irrational and infernal; but it was not very much worse than the mad, destructive fury inspired by John Knox's 'excellent' sermons, which, whatever their merits, can scarcely have emanated from a mind that had any clear comprehension of the processes by which spiritual truth makes its way and holds its power effectively among mankind. Beaton and Knox were both powerful in their age and characteristic of it, but they would have found no conspicuous function in an age that was not in the course of emerging from the mire of savagery, with all its tendencies to violence and to vice. Both alike were uncompromising enemies of individual freedom, and equally bent upon the suppression of all conscientious opinions that did not concur with their own. Both were patriots, and of signal service to Scotland; but the evil they did so nearly counterbalances all the good they did (which might, and would, in time have been done by less unscrupulous, ungentle instruments), that it might have been well had Scotland been liberated by Providence from the piebald burden of both of them.[9]

Buchanan as a scholar was a very large inheritor of the wisdom of many ages, the largest inheritor of that rare kind of wealth of all the Scotsmen of his day. He was by nature somewhat of a sceptic, the teacher in Latin—and who can tell what beside?—of Montaigne—most candid and sincere of sceptics—by necessity a doubter, as true seekers of truth, especially in dark, troubled, fermenting ages, cannot help being. He was a philosopher—a Stoic probably, as most impecunious philosophers are compelled to be more or less, capable of bearing the inevitable with patience, and of waiting to solve difficulties by skill and cautious experiment rather than by violence or deceit! What his worldly wisdom and great intellectual power might have done for the good of his country opens up a wide field of conjecture touching the solution of most of the big problems of his age. Why should the clever, beautiful Queen Mary not have trusted him as an adviser rather than Scotch rakes and traitors and Italian fiddlers? Why should her race, more gifted than most royal races, have hugged a delusion about the Divine right of kings along the precipices overhanging death and ruin? Why should the Reformers, who had the means of ascertaining that among them he was a veritable Saul among the prophets, and neither a fanatic nor a hypocrite, not have utilised his wisdom and his inspiration of the beautiful and the true to direct the course and shape the limits of the Reformation, without proclaiming a barbarian, everlasting divorce between the power of truth and the beauty of holiness? Why should the spiritual force and illumination of every great man who did not wear fine raiment and fare sumptuously every day, of the prophets of Judæa and the sages of Greece and Rome, have been lost upon their contemporaries and left to find its way and its expanding efficacy in the slow course of centuries? Buchanan's lot was the common lot of unendowed, and therefore unappreciated, genius. The greatest scholar and writer of his own country in his own time, one of the most potent of the intellectual aristocracy of Europe for all time, he was a rustic in dress, a plain, unpretentious, non-assertive inhabitant of the European villages called cities, known to him as St. Andrews and Edinburgh; a man pure of life in a vicious, half-decent age; loyal to truth so far as it was possible for him to discover it among contemporaries prone to falsehood and ready for the perpetration of it by forgery or any other effective and not unpracticable mode, he was esteemed a stranger in his native land, and not a Solon or a seer except by the more cultured of his own unlettered generation; to subsequent vulgar generations he was so unknown or so forgotten as to fill, in their rude Temple of Fame, the niche of a mythical court-jester and coarse wit or witling; nevertheless he holds a title to lasting remembrance as sure as the story of the Reformation and the era of the never-to-be-forgotten Mary Stuart can give; also the unique distinction of being the greatest master of the Latin language since it died as a vernacular, and became the immortal medium of intercommunication for the wide, high, and cold republic of scholars and thinkers, scattered through realms of ether and cloudland, and lit by volcanic fire and spiritual aurora fitfully lifting the night from peaks of rock and ice.

FOOTNOTES

[1] When I first heard from one of my early schoolmasters the mediæval chestnut, *Quid distat inter sotum et Scotum? — Mensa tantum.* ('What divides a sot (fool) from a Scot? — Only the table') — the reply was credited to Buchanan.

[2] He was Buchanan's assistant, and called the king's 'Pedagogue,' Buchanan being called 'Master.'

[3] Certain emoluments arising to the feudal superior (in this case the king); which, as they depend on uncertain events, are termed casualties.

[4] This covers the meaning more accurately than 'Physicians.'

[5] Burns appears to have afterwards written it down thus: —

> 'The Solemn League and Covenant
> Now brings a smile, now brings a tear;
> But sacred Freedom, too, was theirs:
> If thou'rt a slave, indulge thy sneer.'

The form may be improved, the sentiment could not be.

[6] My authority is Herkless's *Cardinal Beaton*, p. 153.

[7] My non-forensic sympathy, but not my full conviction, goes with Mr. Hosack and Sir John Skelton in their chivalrous but too unmeasured defence of Mary. My verdict in regard to her being 'art and part' in putting an end to that traitor in heart and deed, the good-for-nothing, faithless fool Darnley, is a hesitant 'Not Proven'; but if otherwise, then a distinct non-hesitant 'served him right.' Skelton's clever, interesting book upon Maitland of Lethington, Mary's most faithful and capable minister, does not throw much, if any, light upon Buchanan. In it he is treated as an opposition pleader, capable rather than scrupulous, who did not know all the facts, and who was instructed by men who had other purposes to serve than telling the whole truth, and who probably did not know it themselves so well as Skelton had opportunities to come to know it, *e.g.* in regard to the 'Casket Letters' — documents that could be satisfactory to no modern tribunal except a Dreyfus court-martial. Buchanan's attack, in a pamphlet written in Scotch, upon Skelton's hero Maitland, entitled *The Chameleon*, Skelton sneers at as a 'Dawb' — not

entirely an inaccurate criticism, for *The Chameleon* is a caricature, and that, of course, means an exaggeration of all faults, actual or presumable. But when a 'chameleon' like Disraeli or Maitland, both of whom have found in John Skelton an ingenious and eloquent hero-worshipper, is assailed by satirists in *Punch* or elsewhere, the only effective condemnatory judgment worth stating is that the caricature is not recognisable by an honest enemy or a free and easy friend. For my part, I believe that the unvarnished truth, though perhaps not the whole of it, can be better inferred from Buchanan than from Skelton.

[8] Sir David Brewster, when Principal of the United College of St. Leonard and St. Salvador, had a residence close to St. Leonard's roofless church. In 1853, Sir David told to a breakfast-party of students, which included Dr. Wallace and the writer, that his house embraced all that existed of Buchanan's old dwelling-house, and pointed out one particular part of the ancient outer wall thick enough to resist the artillery of Buchanan's day. Dr. Johnson's general contempt for Scotland, which did not keep silence in St. Andrews, could not resist the inspiration of the *genius loci* of St. Leonard's so far as to prevent his generously recognising Buchanan's claim to immortality as being as fair as modern Latinity can give, and 'perhaps fairer than the instability of vernacular languages admit.'

[9] Carlyle's estimate of Knox I accept and credit as the estimate of as penetrating an insight and as true a conscience as ever uttered the verdicts of history; but it is the estimate of a mind that could discover more to approve in the storm than in the sunshine, and who too readily infers noble motives from splendid results. I believe all the good he imputes to Knox and his life-battle for truth, and I don't believe sufficiently in the vileness of human nature to believe in any of the charges of immorality which rival ecclesiastics have persisted in relating against him. But for all that, I am not blind to his human imperfections. I am far from thinking him to be a perfect man, much less a perfect Christian. His wild joy and unbridled merriment over the dying miseries of Cardinal Beaton and of Mary of Guise would be scarcely in harmony with the budding benevolence of a half-reformed cannibal. His virtues were genuine, and not hypocritical, but they were essentially Pagan virtues—gifts of nature, tested and strengthened, but not acquired, through his experiences as a notary and an ecclesiastic.

INDEX